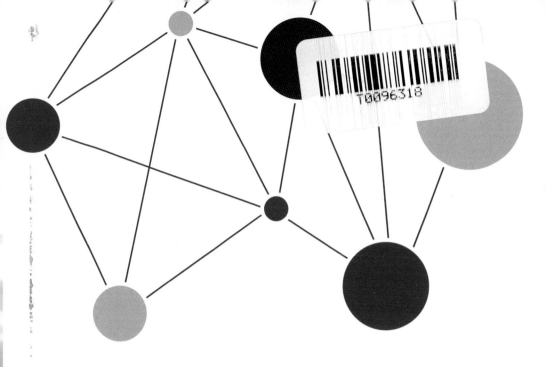

THE HIGH PERFORMANCE MINDSET

AT WORK, HOME AND LIFE

Michael E. Bernard PhD

This book is dedicated to Patricia Bernard for her advice, direction, interest and support.

A very special thanks to Michelle Beecroft, Director, Shell Graphix, for her very thoughtful creative design of this book - and patience!

First published 2021 by Wilkinson Publishing Pty Ltd
ACN 006 042 173
Wilkinson Publishing
PO Box 24135, Melbourne, VIC 3001, Australia
Ph: +61 3 9654 5446
info@wilkinsonpublishing.com.au
www.wilkinsonpublishing.com.au

Book design by Shell Graphix
Printed and bound in Australia by Ligare Pty Ltd.

ISBN: 9781925927542

A catalogue record for this book is available from the National Library of Australia

ABOUT THE AUTHOR

Michael E. Bernard, Ph.D. is an international consultant to universities, organisations, educational authorities and governments. Since 2004, he has been a Professorial Fellow at the University of Melbourne, Melbourne Graduate School of Education and is an Emeritus Professor, California State University, Long Beach. He is the Founder of You Can Do It! Education (youcandoiteducation.com.au) a program for promoting student social-emotional well-being and achievement that is being used in over 6,000 schools in Australia, New Zealand, Vietnam, Singapore, England, Romania and North America.

- Michael was the first sport psychologist of the Collingwood Football Team.

- He is the author of 50+ books, 30+ book chapters, and 30+ journal articles in areas associated with student wellbeing and achievement, peak performance, resilience and positive parenting.

- With his business partner and wife, Patricia Bernard, he has created an online positive parenting program consisting of eLearning programs, articles and audio-video motivational programs for young people (youcandoiteducation.com.au/parents).

- He has worked as a consultant school psychologist helping families and schools address the educational and mental health needs of school-age children.

- A co-founder of the Australian Institute for Rational Emotive Behaviour Therapy and is the author of many books on REBT.

- Over the past decade, he has focused on the design and conduct of high performance mindset and resilience professional development programs.

ALSO BY MICHAEL BERNARD

Procrastinate Later! How to Motivate Yourself to Do It Now

The Successful Mind at School, Study and Life

The Successful Mind at Study, Work and Life

Staying Rational in an Irrational World

Taking the Stress Out of Teaching

You Can Do It! How to Boost Your Child's Achievement in School

Program Achieve. A Social-Emotional Learning Curriculum

Rationality and the Pursuit of Happiness. The Legacy of Albert Ellis

Investing in Parents: What Parents Need to Know and Do to Support Their Children's Achievement and Social-Emotional Well-Being

The You Can Do It! Little Book for Parents (with Patricia Bernard)

How to Be a Successful Young Person (with Patricia Bernard)

You Can Do It! What Every Student (and Parent) Should Know About Achieving Success at School and in Life (with Darko Hajzler)

Rational-Emotive Therapy with Children and Adolescents: Theory, Treatment Strategies, Preventative Methods (with Marie Joyce)

Coaching for Rational Living: Theory, Techniques and Applications (with Oana David)

Advances in REBT. Theory, Practice, Research, Measurement, Prevention and Promotion (with Windy Dryden)

REBT with Diverse Problems and Populations (with Windy Dryden)

Clinical Applications of Rational-Emotive Therapy (with Albert Ellis)

Cognitive-Behavioral, Rational-Emotive Approaches to the Problems of Childhood (with Mark Terjesen)

TESTIMONIALS

"Dr. Michael Bernard has put achievable success and high performance within anyone's reach by clearly demonstrating how removing your self-sabotaging blocks is the direct path to excellence. His bottom line approach makes for not only a terrific read, but can also become the 'reference book' you go back to whenever you encounter an obstacle that stands in your way. I recommend it highly for anyone committed to operating at his or her best!"
Michael S. Broder, Ph.D., Clinical Psychologist, author of Seven Steps To Your Best Life, Philadelphia, Pennsylvania USA

"Dr. Bernard's thinking and his program are eminently sensible based on sound principles of psychology."
London Times, ENGLAND

"This book is a unique resource. Michael Bernard is the pioneer of this field and, based on his lifetime effort, manages to connect the theory, practice, and recent advancements in the psychotherapy, clinical sciences, and positive psychology. In this book, he offers a comprehensive and truly integrative structure for the understanding of human mind, well-being, and productivity, complimented with guidance for the practice and inspiring examples from his own life and work."
Oana Alexandra David, Ph.D. Associate Professor, Department of Clinical Psychology and Psychotherapy, Babes-Bolyai University Cluj-Napoca, ROMANIA

"Michael Bernard's program helped increase the confidence and performance of many of our players."
John Birt, Former football manager, Collingwood Football Club, Melbourne AUSTRALIA

"This book epitomises Michael's strengths as a writer, thinker and practitioner. It is well structured, clear and full of thoughtful ideas of how people can use what Michael terms 'A High Performance Mindset' at their workplace, at home and in their life in general. This book will become a classic and will be referred to for many years to come."
Windy Dryden, Professor, Goldsmiths College, University of London, ENGLAND

"Michael Bernard draws on a lifetime of research, experience and personal wisdom to present a vast suite of strategies and practices that will ensure that you can proactively and successfully negotiate your life journey. By drawing on evidenced-based sciences, in this life-manual, Bernard shows that we can overcome challenges and obstacles through approaches that are available to all of us."
Jim Watterston, Dean, Melbourne Graduate School of Education, The University of Melbourne, AUSTRALIA

"Michael's wise words make this book essential reading for us all as he shines a light on the most important elements of success, happiness and wellbeing in all avenues of life. Practical, insightful and backed by his life's work as a world renowned educational psychologist and even more importantly as a loving husband, father and friend he cuts through to what matters most. This book is a must read for every member of every family."
Heather Leary, Principal, Benalla 31 Primary School, Benalla, Victoria, AUSTRALIA

CONTENTS

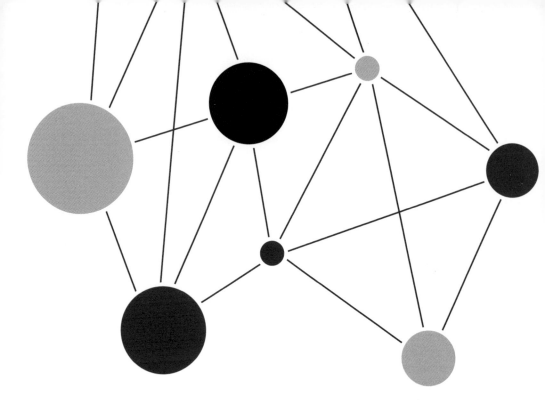

Part 1

Mindset Matters

BEGINNINGS

I have been fortunate to have developed early in my adult life a disciplined work mindset that has helped me achieve many of my work goals which continue to be helping people of all ages overcome barriers to their success and happiness in order to achieve their potential in all areas.

In my work, I am a risk taker. I am extremely determined. I am optimistic. I work long hours and setbacks spur me on. I know I learn from experience and, hopefully, I am getting smarter. And I use my sense of humour not only to connect with others, but to deal with times when the going gets tough.

As a parent of two children (now grown up), I have also been passionate in wanting to do the best I can for them. This has not only included loving my children very hard, but also being as effective as I can be in doing and saying the things that have helped teach them to have good character, to have high levels of social and emotional intelligence in order to be able make the most of their natural potential. My wife has played a big role in this.

As an only child, I have slowly learnt that my very strong drive and determination to be the best at work as a professional as well as raising a happy family and feeling satisfied and fulfilled needs to be combined with an appreciation and connectedness with others. I have learnt that reaching out to and staying connected helps me to thrive as an individual.

And in recent years, I have also learnt about the importance of being committed to my own self including my physical health and emotional well-being. Healthy eating and exercise, accepting myself (and others) unconditionally no matter what happens and having a positive focus are attitudes that are front and centre on my life's radar screen.

Years ago, I read the writing on the wall. I realised that in this irrational world we work in and bring kids up in that when the going gets tough, I needed to take charge of myself because no one around me or who I work for was going to protect or rescue me or solve my problems. I realised that I needed to learn how to be resilient and confident in order to protect myself from the many muddles and puddles in life and to respond positively to tough situations.

I have long realised that every day when I wake up through the time I go to sleep that my own attitudes are the keys that determine how I think, what I feel and how I act. I have learnt and agree with Shakespeare that things are neither good nor bad but thinking makes it so. For sure!

And underpinning my outlook on life is the time-proven serenity prayer that continues to help me get through the tough times I still experience with my family, friends, my work and which threaten my satisfaction in life: "Grant me the serenity to accept those things that I cannot change, the courage to change those that I can and the wisdom to know the difference."

In this book, I have combined the lessons from my own life with proven and practical ideas from different areas of research from the fields of psychology and education which I call on in my roles as coach, consultant and counsellor/therapist.

I promise you that you will find new ideas in this book that will benefit you and that you can apply at work, home and in your life.

PSYCHOLOGY

Across the ages, psychology has concerned itself with studying mental health problems and disorders of people – depression, anxiety, conduct disorders – and how the mind operates at its worst.

A lot has been discovered about the causes of mental health disorders.

We now have explanations of why people experience mental health problems including but not limited to their DNA, family upbringing, surrounding environment and their resultant mental outlook.

At the University of Wisconsin (Madison) I elected to study psychology. I received my masters and doctorate (PhD) in educational psychology. I felt that studying the science of what makes young (and older) people tick would help me to understand and support their challenges, difficulties and to help them solve problems.

My first full-time job was as a lecturer in the Faculty of Education at the University of Melbourne. I was able to spend three days a week working in schools as an educational/school psychologist. I was referred all sorts of students by teachers and parents – those with anxiety, early-stage depression, anger-conduct disorders, learning difficulties. I worked with individual students as well as the significant adults in their lives. I learnt a lot while I, hopefully, helped a lot.

Michael Bernard with Albert Ellis

The counselling approach I employed and continue to use is Rational Emotive Therapy, now called Rational Emotive Behavior Therapy (REBT). REBT was developed by the world famous psychologist, Albert Ellis. He became my mentor and using REBT I helped people to manage their emotions and behaviours by restructuring their irrational beliefs to rational ones. In REBT, young people are taught that while they might not have much power over who they live with and some of the things that happen to them, they have tremendous power over the way they think – a tremendously empowering, mind-opener for many!

I have always been very impressed with the insights and methods of REBT. I co-founded the Australian Institute for Rational Emotive Therapy (with my colleague, Ian Campbell).

Much of my work has been shaped and sharpened by my association with Albert Ellis and many of his insightful ideas appear throughout this book. Over the years I have written and edited many books on REBT.

Positive psychology

Since the year 2000, psychology has turned its attention from understanding and treating mental health problems, to the positive dimension of human functioning contributing to high levels of well-being and fulfilment in life. Many of us have been keen to understand what elements of our inside world contribute to the very highest levels of well-being, some call thriving or flourishing.

Martin Seligman, the founder of modern-day positive psychology has helped us understand what he has called the gold standard of well-being (PERMA). People who flourish demonstrate high levels of Positive Emotions, Engagement, Relationships, Meaning and Accomplishment.

In the accompanying Flourishing Tree, you will observe three commitments (success, others, self) on the trunk that together help you experience the different aspects of PERMA (red apples). Hanging from the three main branches of the tree are attitudes that when put into practice strengthen your commitments. You will also notice that underground beneath the tree are the social and emotional nutrients (resilience) that provide the tree with the strength to overcome obstacles and to grow tall.

The Flourishing Tree

'Growing the well-being of individuals and community'

Relationships 'Caring and giving to others'

Respect

Acceptance of others

Feedback

Engagement 'Being in the zone during absorbing activities'

Empathy

Meaning 'Belonging to something bigger than yourself'

Support

Self-direction

Growth mindset

Self-acceptance

Authenticity

Positive self-regard

Positive Emotions 'Happiness, few negative emotions'

Healthy living

Optimism

Creativity

Positive focus

High Frustration Tolerance

Accomplishment 'Successful achievement of tasks'

S U C C E S S

O T H E R S

S E L F

COMMITMENTS

NUTRIENTS

PERSISTENCE

CONFIDENCE

RESILIENCE

ORGANISATION

RELATIONSHIPS

BRAIN SCIENCE AND NEUROPLASTICITY

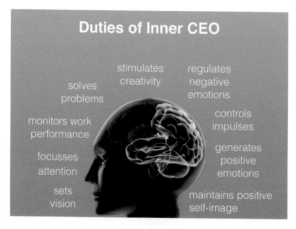

Duties of Inner CEO

stimulates creativity
regulates negative emotions
solves problems
controls impulses
monitors work performance
generates positive emotions
focusses attention
sets vision
maintains positive self-image

Through extensive brain research including use of neuro-imaging techniques, an *inner chief executive officer* has been discovered that determines the extent to which we operate at an optimum level. The inner CEO is located in a brain area of the frontal lobes called the pre-frontal cortex, an area of the brain high up in the cerebral cortex sitting just above our eyes. This part of the brain that has been called an "evolutionary masterpiece" is the last part of the brain to develop.

Our inner CEO engages in an amazing array of important duties. For example, by deciding to more actively monitor the routine, automatic ways we perform our work using data, we are better at changing aspects of our work performance.

Keep in mind that your inner CEO performs some of these duties better than others.

A final point on brain science has to do with the concept called *neuroplasticity* which describes a process where our brains, including our pre-frontal cortex, continue to change and grow throughout the entirety of one's life.

Here's one way our brain becomes smarter. We learn about a new way of thinking, feeling and doing – such as you'll find in this book. The more we repeat what we have learnt and use it, we grow and reinforce a new neural pathway leading to changes in how our brain works.

Neuroplasticity is the "muscle building" part of the brain; the things we do often we become stronger at, and what we don't use fades away. That is the physical basis of why engaging a new thought or action over and over again increases its power. Over time, it becomes automatic; a part of us. We literally become what we think and do.

What I have learned is that when I put a new learning into practice over a 30-day period and I see the benefits, I start to see small changes in me, my being. And over the years continuing to today, I become stronger and more powerful to deal with what comes my way.

What leads to success in business and in life is not controlled so much by outside factors

Everything you need to succeed is within you now.

You are in charge of awakening your inner CEO.

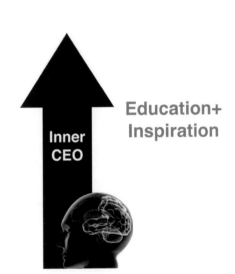

Education+
Inspiration

MINDSET DISCOVERED

Since the year 2000, mindset has been studied scientifically. Here's what we now know.

Our mindset, whether negative or positive, is the lens we use to perceive, interpret and evaluate our world. It shapes our goals, our attitude towards work and relationships and ultimately predicts whether or not we will fulfil our potential. Our mindset towards adversity and tough situations has also been shown to determine the amount of stress we experience.

Stress-is-Negative Mindset vs. Stress-is-Positive Mindset

The extent to which someone has the mindset that stress has positive consequences ("stress-is-enhancing mindset") or holds the mindset that stress has debilitating consequences ("stress-is-debilitating") impacts an individual's performance and productivity, health and wellbeing, learning, growth and life satisfaction.

We know that people's mindset about stress when negative can be altered – to great benefit. In a short period of time, people who learn how to re-frame stress in terms of positive rather than negative effects experience a beneficial effect on their work performance and wellbeing.

Fixed Mindset vs. Growth Mindset

In a 'growth' mindset, people believe that their most basic qualities (including their intelligence, abilities, competencies and worth) can continually be enhanced and developed with effort and practise. As a consequence, they actively enjoy opportunities to learn and improve – to become more competent – even at the risk of appearing to others as less than perfect at something. The confidence levels of "growth" mindset individuals are therefore robust.

In a "fixed" mindset, people believe that their basic qualities are carved in stone and that mistakes mean these qualities are somehow inadequate. People with a fixed mindset often avoid opportunities to improve their skills and abilities, because they don't expect their effort would make any difference to their success. Self-confidence in this mindset is fragile and requires constant success and praise to maintain it.

Mindset: The Big Picture

Since mindset was first studied, we have learnt a lot. Based on current science, this book sheds light on the very latest findings as to the essential qualities of mindset that helps all of us perform at our best, maintain and increase our wellbeing in order to meet the many challenges we face today. I have tried to be comprehensive covering the many aspects of mindset that we all need to manage and prosper at home, work and life. From experiences in my personal and work life that I write about, you will observe the power of mindset to make a big difference.

WHAT DRIVES HIGHEST WORKPLACE PERFORMANCE?

Since 2000, positive psychology research has revealed four types of "capital" (assets, resources) that influence high performance in the workplace.

Economic capital includes financial, tangible assets and has received the most attention as the factor most responsible for high performance.

Human capital refers to job experience, educational qualifications, as well as job skills and knowledge of people working at all levels of the organisation.

Social capital refers to the range and quality of your relationships, network and friends.

The fourth asset that contributes to high performance and well-being is *Psychological capital* – who you are as a person – including but not limited to your self-belief, optimism, hope and resilience. Now as is shown below, all four types of capital contribute to different outcomes at work – the more you have, the higher your success and well-being.

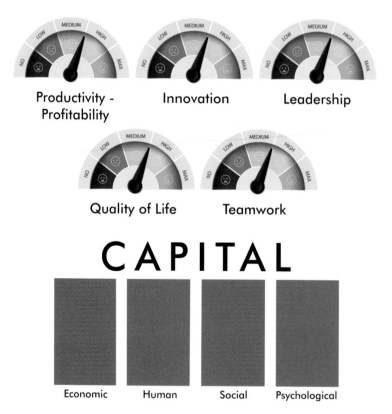

CAPITAL

Recently, research has shown one of the four types of capital takes people and organisations from good to to great – psychological capital.

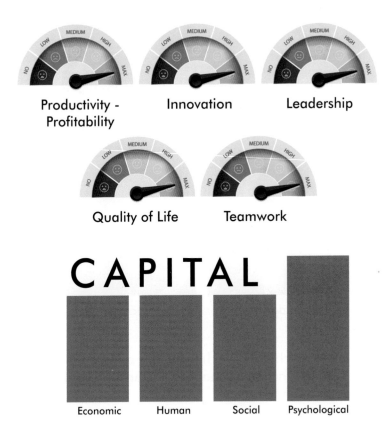

In this book, I shall describe the psychological capital we can all use to help us in various areas of our lives. Through the completion of surveys you'll be able to gain greater awareness of your strengths and areas you'd like to develop further. And there will be plenty of suggestions for how to go about doing this.

BLOCKERS TO HIGH PERFORMANCE

feeling angry

feeling worried

feeling down

procrastination

From research in psychology, we have learnt quite a bit about aspects of people's mental functioning that are like anchors to their ship as they progress through life.

I have focused a lot of my work on helping people of all ages to become more aware of common social-emotional difficulties that are to greater or lesser extents everybody's road to success and happiness including: anxiety, feeling down, anger and procrastination.

The great news is that everyone, anyone, can learn ways to overcome social-emotional blockers – to get them off your road to becoming the person you want to become!

PROFESSIONAL SPORT

Nowhere is a high performance mindset more important than in professional sport.

I cut my teeth on high performance and the blockers to high performance during my time as the first sport psychologist at the Collingwood Football Club.

I was hired by the team's football manager to help motivate several under-performing players who should have been superstars.

I spent a great deal of time attending training sessions and games, spoke with the players as a group and conducted 1:1 mental skills training sessions with over half the team.

> "What happens above the shoulders is more important than what happens below the knees in taking players from good to great."
>
> Mark Williams,
> Captain of Collingwood,
> Premier Coach,
> Port Adelaide

During this time, I witnessed first-hand the pressures and stresses of playing professional sport. I experienced first hand how detrimental stress can be to peak performance.

I remember one of Collingwood's star players telling me how on big game days, when he took a mark and looked towards the goal posts, the actual distance between the goal posts shrunk in size (in his own mind) making it doubly hard to kick the ball straight between the posts.

I also learnt a huge amount about a high performance mindset from Collingwood's true superstars – none bigger and better than captain and now coach, Nathan Buckley. Bucks played with the highest performance mindset possible – as a player. When he was appointed captain, the mindset he needed to captain and lead a team of individuals changed from one with individual success being the goal, to team success and helping individuals realise their potential.

So, here's a few things that I learnt from my time at Collingwood about a high performance mindset.

1. Many elite players have a negativity bias after their team loses or they play poorly; they over-focus on the negative aspects of their play, not what went well.

2. Helping players become aware of internal blockers to playing performance and providing them with the self-management tools results in an improvement not only in their playing performance, but in their capacity to deal with stress and to flourish.

3. Having players set individual goals for what they want to achieve in training and in the following game increases the likelihood that they play better.

4. Teaching players about the difference between negative and positive self-talk and impact on their approach to training and game day made a big difference to many.

5. Collingwood suffered from what was called at the time "Colliwobbles". Colliwobbles is a specific term for choking when it is done by the Collingwood Football Team. Working on the collective mindset of the Collingwood team where we addressed the blocker of anxiety (fear of failure, ridicule) and building up confidence and persistence helped break the spell of the Colliwobbles.

FINANCIAL REVIEW

Home   National   Opinion   World   Business   Technology   Markets   Personal Finance

How to build a champion workforce

PUBLISHED: 14 AUG 2013 00:05:00 | UPDATED: 14 AUG 2013 06:59:36

Nathan Buckley is an example of an individual who exhibits that high-performance mindset in spades.   Photo: Vince Caligiuri

MICHAEL BERNARD

As the first sports psychologist to work for the Collingwood Football Club, I know first hand the mindset required from each player – and coach – for the team to achieve success.

Former captain and Collingwood coach Nathan Buckley is an example of an individual who exhibits that high-performance mindset in spades. You might be surprised to learn that for Buckley that was not always the case.

Through understanding the importance of having an open mind, he continued to learn. Along the way, "Bucks" saw the importance of not wasting time worrying about what has been or what will be; his focus became the here and now.

He learned to be a good listener and the importance of continuously setting and achieving higher and higher goals. He gradually developed the belief he could be as good as he wanted to be – if he was prepared to do the work.

What do our decision makers need to know in order to build high performing mindsets like that of Nathan Buckley in the workforce? Here are four of the factors which give individuals and organisations a competitive advantage.

Economic capital including financial, tangible assets has historically been considered the most important for high performance. However, in the new economy, intangible assets are increasingly being recognised for their sizable contribution.

As organisations strive to do more with less, human capital (job experience, qualifications, job skills and knowledge) have become integral to individual and organisational success.

PSYCHOLOGICAL CAPITAL

A further intangible asset is social capital meaning the size and quality of the networks of people at all levels within and outside an organisation that help individuals solve problems and provide guidance and expertise.

The most important asset is psychological capital. The psychological strengths of a high-performance mindset include such capabilities as self-direction, optimism, high frustration tolerance, empathy, self-acceptance and authenticity.

People who perform at their best are deeply committed not only to their own success, but also to the success and well-being of others. Top performers possess highly developed behavioural strengths which enable them to perform positively and efficiently in managing highly complex, demanding tasks and dealing with difficult people.

To instill that mindset, management and human resource departments need to commit to building the psychological capacity of their workforce.

The extent to which high-performing organisations outperform low-performing organisations on indicators such as effective leadership, productivity, engagement, innovation and well-being, depends on the distribution of the high-performance mindset across employees at all levels of the organisation. The good news is these capabilities can be strengthened not only in professional athletes, but in everyone. It can make the difference between a successful performance or the "Collywobbles".

Professor Michael Bernard is an author, consultant and teacher at Melbourne University.

The Australian Financial Review

YOU CAN DO IT! EDUCATION

ONLINE SOCIAL AND EMOTIONAL LEARNING PROGRAMS

Resilience | Confidence | Persistence | Organisation | Getting Along

Over the past two decades, I have devoted myself, along with my wife and business partner Patricia, and colleagues to helping schools change. Through the year 2000, most schools viewed the academic curriculum as front and centre of their mission. Programs that addressed the social-emotional aspects of young people's development were secondary in priority to the academic purpose and were seen as meeting the needs of students with greatest need.

My good friend and school principal – Heather Leary, and I over two decades ago asked schools to draw and cross a line in the sand to where academics and social-emotional learning were central to the education of all young people. Many schools have responded and the Australian national curriculum now mandates the teaching of personal and social capabilities for students 4–16 years of age.

I continue to write books and develop social-emotional learning curricula. In Australia, You Can Do It! Education (youcandoiteducation.com.au) can be seen in thousands of schools from the early years through the first years of university. And our programs are now being taught in many different countries.

You Can Do It! Education's Success Worldwide

What is also abundantly clear is that social and emotional education of young people is most effective when there is a school-home partnership. We have written material and developed parent education workshops to inform and up-skill parents in the important role they play in developing the positive attitudes and social-emotional skills of their children.

In 2018 we launched an online positive parent education program consisting of skill-based video programs and article for parents (youcandoiteducation.com.au/parents).

It's all in THE MIND

How do you transform an underachiever with potential to a high performer?

by MICHAEL E. BERNARD

As the first sport psychologist of the Collingwood Football Club, I cut my teeth on the challenge of converting significant potential to high performance. I worked with four talented coaches, leaders of the Magpie tribe. I helped senior coaching staff (and players) come to see that what occurs above the shoulders of elite athletes is as important as what takes place below the knees.

All players participated in pre-season learning and development programs designed to strengthen their psychological capacity or mindset. This initiative enhanced their playing performance as well as their ability to cope with tough situations and to manage stress, including helping to overcome what used to be called the Colliwobbles. I worked with many individual players during the week and immediately before and after a game.

Strengthening the mental approach of highly talented athletes often makes a big difference to their performance. This principle also applies to helping develop the leadership potential of those who work in any job sector.

Through these experiences and working with a variety of educational and business organisations, I am now absolutely convinced that the capacity of people at all levels in an organisation to perform at their best is enhanced when they know more about how their mind operates at its best – and at its worst – and this is where HR learning and development can play a significant role.

THE HR CHALLENGE

Today, HR continues to expand its role in supporting new business strategy as well as increasing employee engagement, innovation and productivity – signature strengths of high-performing workplaces. It's my view that the HR role can be enhanced through learning and development that focuses on strengthening the psychological capacities and the high-performance mindset of leaders, managers and, ultimately, of the total workforce. Such efforts have important bottom-line benefits including:

- Accelerated business/organisational strategy execution
- Greater ROI on learning and development initiatives (more people applying what they learn to produce concrete and worthwhile results)
- Development of strengths of leaders, managers and employees in an organisation's competency framework
- Increased employee positivity and capacity to cope with change

Case Study 1

Several football players I worked with were inconsistent in kicking for goal, partly because of what appeared to be internal, mental distractions as they lined up to kick the ball. Their self-talk was distracting, leading to anxiety and rapid loss of confidence: "What if I miss? I'm not kicking straight today. I've forgotten how to kick a goal." Some players did not appear to know what to think, or that they had choices in what to think. One player needed help focusing his attention when kicking for goal. Together, we developed a short phrase – turn around, relax, kick – that helped him to narrow his focus and feel confident. "Before each game, he would ask me for a reminder card with those words written on it, which he would wear in his sock during the game. Focused-attention training combined with confidence-building self-instruction resulted in increased goal kicking.

EVIDENCE CLEARLY SHOWS THAT WHAT OCCURS ABOVE THE SHOULDERS IS AS IMPORTANT, OR SOMETIMES MORE IMPORTANT, THAN THE TECHNICAL SKILLS OF THE JOB.

enablers – they provide people with the self-belief, desire and energy needed to engage in high-impact leadership behaviours.

Thanks to the ground-breaking work of Professor Fred Luthans of the University of Nebraska, we know there are four types of capital (assets or resources) that are associated with individual and organisational workplace performance indicators such as productivity-profitability, engagement, innovation, quality of life (wellbeing at work) and leadership.

Economic capital
finances, tangible assets

Human capital
job experience, education, skills

Social capital
relationships, networks, friends

Psychological capital
confidence, resilience, persistence

Serious investment by organisations in developing the psychological capabilities of leaders and managers at all levels is more the exception than the rule. Decision makers are used to investing in technical skills development to solve existing problems and increase capacity. Therefore, the case needs to be argued by HR that evidence (research and case studies) clearly shows that what occurs above the shoulders is as important, or sometimes more important, than the technical skills of the job.

Here are three important points that can be made when arguing the case to senior management and executive leadership that growing leadership capacity of people results in higher performing workplaces.

The extent to which people consistently and effectively demonstrate high-impact leadership behaviour and display effective styles of leadership depends on their psychological capabilities and the extent to which they possess a high-performance mindset.

People who display effective leadership style and positive leadership behaviour are those who have well-developed psychological capacity. Without well-developed psychological capacity, it is much harder for people to develop as leaders and demonstrate leadership behaviour. Said another way, psychological capabilities are behavioural

The more your organisation possesses of each type of capital, the higher the levels of workplace performance.

Which of the four types of capital listed above do you think provides the competitive advantage that takes individuals and organisations from good to great? If you think psychological capital, you are on the money.

Leaders vary in terms of the development of a high-performance mindset. Some have a highly developed capacity to work hard, but display areas of under-development related to their relationships with others. And some, because they do not look after themselves or have a negative bias in the way they view the world, are prone to ill health and burnout.

Many studies reveal the robust relationship between a high-performance mindset and better job performance and resilience. It also allows for reduced stress, higher motivation and commitment and increased levels of job and life satisfaction.

AHRI offers a course on building resilience in the workplace. For more information, visit www.ahri.com.au/resilience.

Michael E. Bernard, PhD, is a psychologist and professor at Melbourne Graduate School of Education, University of Melbourne. He is the author of more than 50 books including: Procrastinate Later! *and* The High Performance Mindset at Work. *Michael Bernard spoke at the AHRI HR Leadership Conference in 2013.*

Case Study 2

John is a highly promising manager of an investment unit in a financial institution who consistently showed large profit margins. However, 12 months ago, he failed in his bid to be promoted to an executive position. The reasons given at the time had to do with the following. While John had great commitment to his own success, his commitment to others' success and wellbeing in his unit was under-developed. Additionally, commitment to himself in terms of positivity and health was a problem. His 360 feedback revealed someone lacking in empathy, respect and authenticity. With John participating in a performance mindset program, he began to view himself and those he worked with differently. He began by losing weight while giving up smoking – no easy feat. He made a point of listening more without offering advice and he showed more interest in those he was leading and for the tasks they were accomplishing. Overall, he has become more accepting, tolerant and much more of a positive person – according to recent feedback from others. He has made changes in his mindset that have resulted in increasing his leadership capacity – and is much more likely to gain promotion.

THE HIGH PERFORMANCE MINDSET FORMULA

This book presents my views based on research and my experiences on how you can strengthen your mindset for high performance.

I have combined all that I know into a simple formula:

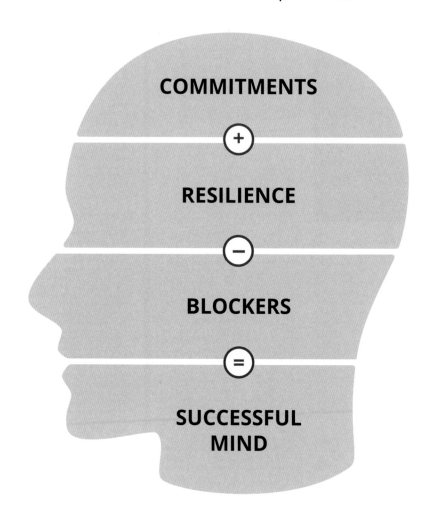

COMMITMENTS

+

RESILIENCE

−

BLOCKERS

=

SUCCESSFUL
MIND

What I have learnt is that there are what I call COMMITMENTS which focus on *success, others and self* that are the very foundations of the mindset of people who are thriving and highly successful in many areas of their lives.

Now, the energy and action that high performers have developed to overcome difficulty and that propel them towards their goals is found in their RESILIENCE. Resilience involves the ability to stay calm and to use different social-emotional skills (confidence, persistence, organisation, getting along) to solve problems, overcome challenges and to go one better.

And as you can see in the formula, a key to a successful mind is the ability to minimise internal BLOCKERS such as anxiety, feeling down, anger and procrastination.

This book shines a light on this formula and through the use of self-surveys and practical strategies, you will be further down the road to having a successful mind.

ONWARDS!

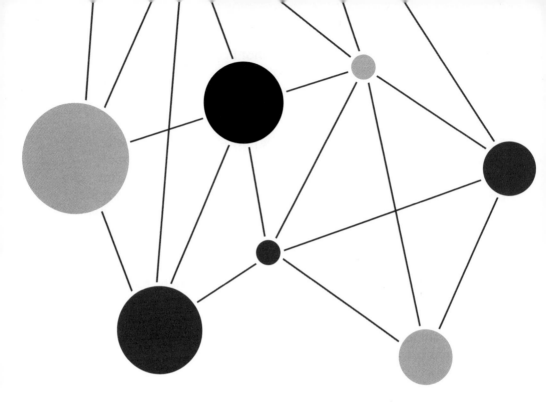

Part 2

Commitments

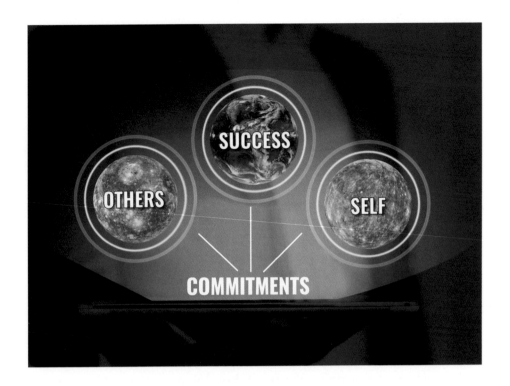

"Commitment unlocks the doors of imagination, allows vision, and gives us the 'right stuff' to turn our dreams into reality."
James Womack, author, *Lean Thinking*

"The quality of a person's life is in direct proportion to their commitment to excellence, regardless of their chosen field of endeavor."
Vince Lombardi, American football coach

"Great organisations demand a high level of commitment by the people involved."
Bill Gates, co-founder Microsoft, philanthropist

"Commitment is the enemy of resistance, for it is the serious promise to press on, to get up, no matter how many times you are knocked down."
David McNally, author, *Even Eagles Need a Push*

"Desire is the key to motivation, but it's determination and commitment to an unrelenting pursuit of your goal – a commitment to excellence – that will enable you to attain the success you seek."
Mario Andretti, highly successful racing driver

WITHOUT COMMITMENT – WE CAN'T ACHIEVE MUCH

When you think about it, just about everything you have accomplished began with a commitment you made; whether it's your family, your education or career. Learning how to commit is not simply about making commitments, it's about keeping those commitments in the face of foreseen and unforeseen hurdles.

What I have learnt is simple. If I want to excel at anything in life, I need to be committed. If I only want to be good enough to get by, then my commitment to excellence is not necessary.

Now, wanting something like having a great relationship, career or healthy life and actually making a commitment to getting it are two different things. I may have big goals that I feel are important, but do I have the determination to see them through?

Being committed is a willingness to do whatever it takes to fulfil and follow through on your plan to reach your goals. It means doing not only what you enjoy doing the most, but doing what you enjoy the least.

Commitments are like signed agreements you have with yourself.

To understand what a commitment is, let's consider New Year's resolutions. Have you ever made a New Year's resolution? Why do we call these decisions or promises to do something we make around New Year's Day 'New Year's resolutions'? We do so because we do not stick to the resolution for very long. That is what they are known for.

While we see the benefit of keeping to the resolution, because of a lack of 100 per cent commitment to it, we break the resolution. We allow ourselves to be influenced by other forces such as peer pressure and even our own rationalisations; for example, "I'll start tomorrow when I'm more in the mood".

Making a commitment is where you pledge yourself to a certain purpose no matter what. We have discovered that some people say they want to be successful, or to get along with others, or to be emotionally and physically healthy. But deep down they are not sufficiently committed to think, feel and act in ways that help to get them where they want to go. It is as though their internal GPS is not yet sufficiently programmed.

Two fundamental conditions underpin being committed: The first is having a sound set of beliefs. There is an old saying: "Stand for something or you'll fall for anything".

The second is faithful adherence to those beliefs through your behaviour. Wavering commitment is no commitment at all. Commitment is most difficult and most readily proven when faced with a tough situation.

The three commitments: Foundations that matter most

Here's a description of the three commitments of people who perform at consistently high levels in these changing and challenging times with a minimum of stress, while maintaining positive relationships and good health. In this book, I will then describe each in greater detail and give you an opportunity to self-assess your own commitments.

Commitment to Success

1. single-minded purpose to be extremely successful at work, home and life

2. focussed concentration on what has to be done to achieve positive outcomes

3. optimism about achieving both short-term and long-term goals

4. responsible risk taking knowing that through mistakes and failures, one develops one's talents and abilities

5. intense determination to make personal sacrifices including short-term fun

6. high tolerance of frustration in order to bring about long-term success

7. creative, open approach to solving problems and willingness to think "out of the box"

8. resilience to bounce back after setbacks and failure

Commitment to Others

1. helping others grow and develop to be the best they can be and overcoming their problems

2. giving including volunteering and not expecting anything back in return

3. respecting people who are different

4. making people feel valued including the tasks they perform

5. empathy towards people experiencing difficulties

6. respect for the differences of opinion and behaviour of people from diverse backgrounds

7. not judging people by their behaviour

8. seeing retaliation for perceived injustice or unfairness as unnecessary and, oftentimes, counter-productive

Commitment to Self

1. healthy lifestyle that includes rest, recreation, relaxation and diet

2. spending quality time with family and friends

3. taking full responsibility for one's own feelings and actions no matter the situation and refusing to blame others

4. accepting oneself as a fallible human being and not judging one's self-worth in terms of one's accomplishments at work or others' opinions

5. being proud of who you are as a person based on your skills, talents, interests and strengths of your family, culture and religion

6. positive focus on situations and one's daily encounters and accomplishments

7. authenticity by standing up for what you believe in and not being afraid to say how you see things and what you believe is right

8. gratitude towards others for what they have contributed to your life

Once you're committed to success, others and self, your mind becomes like a homing beacon. There are no more choices to be made, just a focus on the target in front of your eyes – smooth sailing and fortitude to deal with stormy waters.

Read through the following case studies of Jimmy Chan and Gina Moriarity both of whom work for the same organisation. Notice how their degrees of commitment differ. Notice how while their educational backgrounds, innate talent and potential for success and wellbeing appears similar, their different mindsets deliver different results.

CASE STUDIES IN CONTRAST: JIMMY CHAN

Male, 35 years of age. Currently manages an investment unit at the Federation Bank. Ambitious and driven, Jimmy prides himself on his ability to turn large profits for the bank. He attended a private school and obtained his degree from a major university majoring in economics and commerce.

Friday morning

Jimmy was feeling good – very good. He was in his harbourside office at 7am gazing out across the bay – something to be said for the trappings of success – hard won as they were. He mentally ticked his way through his list of critical achievements over the last four years. Increased profit margins to the tune of five per cent, more and bigger clients, a steady stream of available high yield investment options and yes it was true, a lucky global environment for someone who worked the way he did.

Sitting at the top of his work unit he was more than ready to take the inevitable next step up to Branch Manager and then the Executive and, eventually, if he was not mistaken, CEO of the State Branch of the Federation Bank, one of the big four bastions of the country's financial system.

He reflected back to when he first started – one of the hungry ghosts or "young turks" as they called them. It had been a strong intake that year with the bank picking from the top of the graduate crop. Jimmy and four others had been selected for a two-year development program and had been attached to operational units to learn the business.

Two of the intake had lasted and two had left for greener pastures. That had left him and Gina Moriarty and for the last year both of them had been managing staff as well as developing the business.

According to Jimmy, Gina was OK but she lacked drive – that was the problem with female executives–they still wanted to spend time with their kids and it always impacted their performance. She was not really a threat to him.

Managing staff was not Jimmy's favourite pastime – so time intensive and, in his opinion, most simply were not driven enough to really add value. Jimmy believed in setting a cracking pace and anyone who could not keep up he considered to be "dead wood" that needed to be cleared out. The hardest ones were the older guys who seemed to think that they knew more than he did. Why then were they not in charge? He was aware that his staff could be critical of him, but with him at the helm they had exceeded all targets and Jimmy was very proud of that.

A natural born achiever Jimmy has always believed in himself and knew he had a big future. Some had tried to curb his self belief but they hadn't stood a chance. He knew what he could and would do with his life.

Jimmy has never been short on ambition and he backed it up with natural brilliance and an almost manic level of application to whatever task he faced. He knew he had been gifted with an excellent brain and as far as he was concerned anything was achievable provided you worked hard – no slacking off or getting distracted. Focus was the key – focus and very careful goal setting. Everything in fact that his father had told him had been true.

Jimmy worked hard and played hard too. He understood the power of the boy's club and he worked it to his advantage as much as possible, with regular late night bar crawls and occasional visits to what he referred to as the Wealth Club. His generally supportive wife, Amy, had trouble with that stuff – why couldn't she see that it was all part of a strategy to get them into the inner sanctum of his city's banking elite? Their two kids were already enrolled for places at one of the state's top grammar schools and Amy never complained about the BMW and their wonderful house so why couldn't she support him without question? She should understand that work had to come first sometimes and if he missed the occasional milestone for the kids then so be it. When they first met he had promised her he would change their lives and as far as he was concerned he had delivered.

Jimmy's stomach twisted and he jolted – damn stomach ulcer playing up again – he quickly downed some Taggart and moved to his desk. Amy nagged him about the ulcer and slowing down but he knew he had to push through it if they were going to get what they wanted – an early retirement preferably on a six-figure income. Last year he had failed to reach the higher level of bonus he had planned on and he had upped the drinking then, too. The last two years had been a little tough on his body and he knew he had been drinking a little too much but after all, he was in a pretty stressful role and everyone occasionally reached their breaking point.

Jimmy still struggled to accept not reaching that particular goal and was pretty self-loathing as a result. He also blamed his manager for not pushing his performance enough with the executive and for making him so angry at times by not giving him the support he needed.

Jimmy glanced at his Rolex and realised that he had been wasting valuable time day dreaming. Time to prepare himself and get into the zone for the meeting – after all, it was almost a foregone conclusion that the job was his. Jimmy was headed for a leadership role in the executive – that had always been the unstated promise and he was more than ready for it.

Friday afternoon

Jimmy felt supremely confident as he waited to be invited into his feedback session. He was aware that a 360 degree had taken place and he was sure that he would have passed that with flying colours. Pity they had surveyed his staff as well as his senior management and clients but he was sure his achievements would speak louder than anything else.

The door opened and George, Director of Corporate Services, smiled and waved Jimmy in. Jimmy was a little surprised to see the Director of HR in there as well as the rest of the executive but long ago Jimmy had mastered the poker face required to be a senior banker.

"Hi Jimmy, good to see you. As you know we are looking at the leadership team for going forward with the strategic business direction and there is no doubt that you have been viewed as a strong candidate for promotion to the executive. That is in fact why we undertook the 360-degree analysis of everyone at your level."

Jimmy blinked; he had not realised that there were others being seriously considered, after all no one had topped his figures.

"As you are aware, Jimmy, strong leadership at Federation Bank is critical to our success and we are looking for a range of qualities and abilities in our executive that will help us to remain competitive and continue to expand the business. So, we are here to have a look at how your performance has been rated by not just your manager, but by staff and clients as well. We have also analysed business results which, by the way are extremely impressive."

Jimmy smiled – this was his strength.

"The results from your area speak for themselves Jimmy – you have improved productivity and met every target we have set and you are to be congratulated on that. It would seem, however, that this success has come at quite a cost and that is what we want to focus on today. Jimmy, you have been managing a team with a mixture of experienced and inexperienced staff. That does not come without its challenges and we have listened carefully to the feedback from your people which, to be honest, is a little disappointing."

Jimmy's jaw twitched involuntarily.

"The feedback from your team is that you are overly controlling and that you do not place a great deal of trust in your staff's ability and corporate knowledge. There is a belief that you think they will make mistakes and so you micromanage them – they also mentioned the fact that they feel pushed to perform to sometimes unreasonable standards and that there is a culture of little real reward and recognition when they meet those standards and exceed set targets. Your staff also seems to believe that you are so set in your style and approach to work that you will not consider any suggestions they make because you are so afraid of being seen by others as making mistakes and not meeting set targets due to trying something new.

"Your team also commented on how you respond when things do not go according to your stated plan. Apparently, there have been at least three occasions when you simply dropped the ball and took time off after openly accusing individuals of incompetence.

"You sometimes seem to avoid any 'discomfort' when obstacles arise. They experienced you as judgmental and sensed that you believed they either 'had it or not'. This was particularly difficult for your older and more experienced team members.

"They reported that you were present at discussions but that they did not feel that you actually listened to them and that the conversation was actually about you seizing every opportunity to tell them what you think. One of your team members said you seemed to lack any empathy for what she was going through when it became known she was having a relationship conflict with another team member. They reported that you are incredibly intelligent but that you became irritated very quickly if you did not think they were fast enough to grasp what you were saying."

"In fact, Jimmy, they said that you communicate pretty directly that they were stupid if they could not present every fact and figure to do with any issue on the spot. They also said that your tone of voice was scathing and your non-verbal cues dismissive. Any comments?"

Jimmy was stunned. How dare they. After all of the work he had put in. Half of them should be retired out and the other half should never have been employed. He leant forward in his chair and responded: "That is interesting feedback considering what we have achieved, and frankly I think it is misguided. Under my management, the staff has increased productivity, worked more hours and brought in more accounts. I do listen to them and I give them the benefit of my expertise and methodology. I think that feedback is churlish to say the least."

George continued, "Apparently, in performance management you have been very critical of anyone who has made any level of error of mistake in process and that you have told them that their errors reflect badly on both you and the unit. One staff member reported receiving an email at 4pm on a Friday afternoon stating that he had failed to meet the requirements of his role and that he had a meeting with you to discuss his lack of performance first thing on Monday morning. At that meeting, you simply focused on the negatives and you did not express any appreciation of his contributions to the team's results and showed a complete lack of positive focus. You even described the lucrative new account he had won as 'what he was paid to do'.

"That client was a great achievement for your unit and the bank Jimmy, but you did not seem to be able to recognise the level of effort and work put in. We depend on our people going the extra yard and we believe in recognising excellence. You seem to have a problem with this. Your team also mentioned that you had no idea about their career aspirations and that there had been a lack of opportunity to attend any professional development activities or to act in any higher duty positions."

By now Jimmy was sweating. This was not going according to his plan. This was not what he had expected or deserved and he was shaken. He was temporarily speechless.

"Staff also reported that they felt like they were expected to be machines at work. They were very aware that you know nothing about their personal lives and that you made it clear that they were here to do their jobs not run a social club. They also felt that you had made no effort to understand their cultures and backgrounds and that you did not place importance on values or cultural beliefs. This was highlighted by the way you responded to Hadassa's needs when she requested leave to attend her grandfather's funeral in Israel."

Now Jimmy was irritated and he spat his response: "That was simply not possible – we had to reinvest a major client's portfolio and I needed Hadassa on deck for that. Her request was unreasonable as she wanted to leave the next day and rabbited on about Jewish traditions. After all it was not like it was her immediate family member was it? Did you expect me to let go of all that work and let the bank down?"

There was silence at this and the panel collectively gazed at Jimmy.

"OK, Jimmy, let's move onto feedback from your direct manager. She has reported that she has had to hassle you to complete monthly budget statements and that you described the network for managers at your level as dull and predictable. She also observed that on several occasions you chose to go out drinking with a group of male senior managers and delegated the budget report to senior staff in your unit. We are a conservative organisation and how staff conduct themselves matters. One client reported having seen you drunk at a club and they felt that this did not reflect well on the organisation."

Jimmy's gut twisted. That night had been in response to an argument with his wife and he had gone out and cut loose. She was always nagging him about spending more time with her and the kids and he had snapped. Just how closely had they been watching him? How much did they know about his personal life?

George sat back and closed Jimmy's personnel file. There was a moment of silence and then he began to deliver his summary statement.

"There is no doubt that you are quite brilliant Jimmy, and that you have added value to the bank's profit margins and we appreciate that a great deal. Your short and long term goal setting has been outstanding and your Commitment to Success is unquestionable. Leadership, however, requires the ability to set a vision and inspire people to go there with you. It is about creating a climate in which people can and will reach their full potential and feel valued and supported on the journey. Jimmy you are faultless with facts and figures but you have a lot to learn about self-awareness, self-management and managing relationships. We have some concerns about your work-life balance and your general health and wellbeing as well. Burn out happens a lot in this industry and we cannot afford the consequences of people dropping in their tracks. So where to from here?

"We have decided to allocate you a mentor from the board and to keep you at this level for the next twelve months and then we will see if there are any improvements or not. And Jimmy, if you have not made any significant improvements we may have to review your contract of employment and make some hard decisions. OK, that's it, thanks and you can go now. And Jimmy, take time to stop and smell the roses – you only live once you know."

Jimmy nodded mutely and stood up. It felt surreal – this could not be happening to him. He looked at the panel one last time and headed for the door – clearly, he had a lot of work to do.

CASE STUDIES IN CONTRAST: GINA MORIARITY

Female, 35 years of age. Currently manages an investment unit at Federation Bank and her key role is to manage the team and build the business through the acquisition of new accounts. She grew up in a small, rural town and moved to a major urban centre to study statistics and economics at a top university. Gina works hard to manage a work life balance and is very committed to learning and development. She has one child and lives in a converted warehouse in an inner-city suburb.

Friday morning

Gina watched as her son Thomas disappeared into the colourful swirling environment. She loved this place – the endless research had paid off and Thomas was thriving at the University's Early Learning Centre. It was hard to leave her son but she knew he was benefiting from the experience. Gina waved one last time and headed for her car. She opened the door, relaxed into the leather seats and hit play filling the car with Bach's Concerto Number 7. She was on her way to Federation Bank where she headed up a team of six staff who worked with her to manage a range of investment accounts for some blue-chip clients.

Gina was proud of her team and proud of their results. They had not only achieved quarterly performance goals, they had consistently improved their service delivery and as a result, they were attracting new and bigger clients. A naturally good people manager, Gina attributed her team's excellent performance to her happy team and her fairly common-sense management style. Gina truly believed in people's potential and her management philosophy was to create an environment within which people could and did excel. This, she knew, required her to treat people as adults and to demonstrate the level of respect for their differences that she herself required to be happy and productive in the workplace.

Gina had worked hard to get where she was. A country girl, Gina had made good in the city. Always voted the most likely to succeed, Gina had inherited her father's discipline of setting goals and seeing them through and being mentally tough when under pressure, putting in whatever effort was required to overcome obstacles rather than allowing obstacles to throw her off course. Even when others were out partying, Gina had refused to be distracted, preferring to miss out now for the longer-term gain. While she accepted that sometimes circumstances beyond her control could temporarily derail her, they could not defeat her. She was (and is today) known for having great energy and could never be described as being lazy.

Her mother was incredibly positive and rational in her outlook and her favourite saying was "thinking makes it so, never blame others Gina, make the right decisions about how to think and everything else just falls in place." Her parents had been surprised at her passion for maths and finance but had only ever encouraged her to pursue her goals and set her sights as high as she could. Gina had "inherited" her mother's optimistic disposition and made a point of never blaming the organisation, management or staff when her moods and/or behaviour were less than perfect. She had learned over time the value of her mother's wisdom and today – Gina is a firm believer in the glass being half full rather than half empty. She also believes that through experience, learning, and feedback from others she continues to get smarter. She also knew the importance of not being afraid to make mistakes and to take responsible risks and she supported her people by training them to not be fearful of trying new and better ways of working.

She had not always been that way. In fact, only seven years ago, Gina had been a different animal, single-minded and driven by work. She had rated her worth according to how successful her business outcomes were. If she lost a deal or inadvertently screwed up a contract she would experience a sense of profound self-loathing and a type of controlled panic. To get over it she would work harder and longer, punishing herself for the error and committing to never ever repeating it. She had set high standards and pursued success since the day she was born.

After graduating with distinctions she had been snapped up by the Federation Bank who had recognised her capacity to lead and influence as well as win accounts. That was when she worked 80-

hour weeks and ran herself into the ground – coffee, cigarettes and alcohol had been her frequent friends and the toll on her body had been horrendous. Finally, stress, high blood pressure and utter fatigue had taken their toll and she had suddenly started to cry and found she could not stop – not for a long time.

That had been a turning point for Gina. She had recognised that she was badly in need of some personal development. She enrolled in a positive psychology course and commenced meditation and yoga to pull her back into alignment and get some inner strength back. She spent more time with friends and family to get her life back into balance. She continues to start every day with an affirmation of all of her best qualities and an acceptance of herself despite her imperfections and a meditation of thanks for all of the good things in her life. At the end of each day, she makes a pointed effort to pick out three things that went well and to focus on them – and she sometimes sends an email or drops a note to someone whose efforts she appreciated.

She also enrolled in a leadership program for women and engaged a life skills coach from whom she learned about the importance of not rating her worth as a person by her job performance. She adopted a reflective practice model and still keeps a learning journal which helps her to stay focused on achieving her goals and being mindful of how she is managing her relationships with both staff and clients.

The traffic began to move, and Gina snapped back into the present. Today was an important day. Today, she had her meeting with the executive to receive her 360 degree feedback but first she had a pile of work to knock over in the morning.

Friday Afternoon

The boardroom door opened and George greeted Gina with genuine warmth. He ushered her into the room and she nodded and smiled at the panel, pleased to note that she knew them all.

"Gina – how good to see you. I am sure you are aware that we are looking at the leadership team for going forward with the strategic business direction and there is no doubt that you have been viewed as a strong candidate for promotion to the executive.

That is, in fact, why we undertook the 360-degree analysis of everyone at your level.

"Let's start with the stats – good performance Gina, you and your team have been setting a new standard for business development and that is impressive. You have increased the overall profit in your area by a consistent four per cent and we are more than happy with that. Every target has been met and many exceeded. Your strategic positioning has been excellent and your goal setting has matched it so well done – good management Gina."

Gina smiled and started to relax a little. She was nervous and she did not want it to show.

"Now let's talk about your team and their feedback." Gina tenses slightly and forces herself to breath from the diaphragm. "Your team was overwhelmingly positive about your management style. One person described you as 'being willing and able to listen and gives me advice not judgement when I am struggling'. Another said you make a point of regularly mentioning something positive to her about her performance. You also arranged for her to join a professional development network and you support her in activities related to that network.

"You had a difficult situation with Mia Davies who was very sick at your busiest time of the year. She advised us that you spent time with her and checked in every few days to see how she was travelling. She said you were amazing in reading her non-verbals and noticed she was low in energy and having difficulty in resuming the workload. You adjusted her work hours and gave her remote access for an additional two weeks. She reported that this made her feel valued as a person and for the tasks she was performing – she attributes her recovery in part to your good management. And then there is Joachim. We all know that he can be short with people and we all know that he has some difficulty at having a female boss. You, however, seem to be able to transcend that and understand that he has been with Federation for over 20 years and that he has lived through some extraordinary corporate changes. He reported that you have always respected his culture and beliefs and that you were able to work with his differences. He said that when he did something that didn't pay off, when you spoke to him, he did not feel you were judging him as a person. He described you as firm but fair and frankly, no one has ever managed to get the level of performance from him that you have – quite an achievement.

"Gina, your clients gave you glowing reports as did your staff and we are very happy with the way you are working. We gave you some tough targets and you took them on but more impressively, you led your team in the process and gave them reward and recognition on the way. You have demonstrated commitment to both yourself and others in the workplace including sophisticated relationship management competencies."

Gina felt as if she was floating – this was seriously good feedback.

"The Federation Bank prides itself on our client and people management capacity. You are exactly the kind of leader we are looking for. You have excellent potential and are committed to creating success for both yourself and your team. You make others feel valued and included and you consistently invest in personal and professional development. We have seen you overcome adversity and make changes when they are needed and you have a strong level of belief in your own abilities without compromising your values. Gina we are offering you a promotion to the executive and we fully expect that you may eventually become a candidate for CEO."

Gina smiled and heard herself say, "It will be an honour to work at that level. I assure you that I will give it my all."

The case study of Gina Moriarity in contrast with Jimmy Chan clearly indicates that the Commitment to Success is necessary but not sufficient for top performance and effective leadership. Today, you have to be equally conscious of the needs and ambitions of the people you work with. You need to make sure you show by your actions and words that you value and support them.

Finally, Jimmy Chan's limited commitment to his own well-being including his lack of positive focus undermined his ambition for promotion and recognition.

"It is commitment that transforms the vision of success into actual success. Commitment stands first on the list of values and priorities of successful people. Being committed thus requires that a person is fully engaged in his/her endeavours and remains conscious and persistent enough to realise his/her goals."
Dr. Pramila Srivastava, author, economist, management consultant

"The road to success is through commitment, and through the strength to drive through that commitment when it gets hard. And it is gonna get hard and you're gonna wanna quit sometimes, but it'll be coloured by who you are, and more who you want to be."
Will Smith, actor

"Unless commitment is made, there are only promises and hopes; but no plans."
Peter F. Drucker, author, *Managing Oneself*

"The level of success you achieve will be in direct proportion to the depth of your commitment."
Roy T. Bennett, author, *The Light in the Heart*

"There's no scarcity of opportunity to make a living at what you love. There is only a scarcity of resolve to make it happen."
Wayne Dyer, author, *Your Erroneous Zones*

Research has shown that the most important key to success is that of making a Commitment to Success. That means that you will have a much better chance of being successful if you make that kind of commitment.

Why does a commitment, which means under all circumstances dedication to overcome obstacles, help you succeed? Because of the way most people's minds work, we feel compelled to honour our commitments, even to ourselves. A commitment creates a powerful force within us. In this case, we are talking about making a commitment to our own success.

Staying committed to your goal is one of the most fundamental principles of success. The goals can vary from leading a healthier life, having a better relationship, or achieving results at work, but commitment remains an essential ingredient.

Of the three commitments I'll be discussing, the Commitment to Success is my strongest and most constant – more so than my Commitment to Others (with the exception of my family) while my Commitment to Self seems to be the area that needs most encouragement.

I am someone who has a long-standing and very strong commitment to being as successful as my native ability and circumstances allow. Said in a slightly different way, my moral purpose in life is to raise my two children in ways that bring out their best – that includes happiness and fulfilment. I'll discuss my parenting approach later in this book. Also, at home, as best I can I try to be a supportive and loving partner to my wife – and we do have a great relationship for 35 years and counting. And as a matter of interest, my kids, too, are doing well – though not without occasional setbacks and challenges.

My friends, family and colleagues will also agree that I have an over-arching desire to be successful in my work – with my passion and determination being fuelled by my desire for my work to make a positive difference in the lives of others – especially young people.

It seems pretty clear to me what has determined my degree of success at work and in relationships with my family has been the extent of my commitment in these areas.

This sounds obvious but it isn't. What I have learnt from countless interviews and coaching experiences is that people are different in what they view as being important to them in life.

Some people view relationships as being central to their existence and they commit themselves to getting along with everyone. In some people's mind, as a senior leader recently wrote on a LinkedIn post, the key to success "is being nice to people".

My view is not dissimilar in some respects. If you are not nice to people, if you bully and treat others without respect, if you have a single-minded determination to win at all costs, you will find it much harder to be successful – especially if you are a manager or senior leader in an organisation (COO, CFO, managing director). Yet without a 100% commitment to your own success and to the success of others (and the organisation you lead or work for), you and those you work with and for will often fall short of achieving a personal or collective personal best.

Looking at this issue from the perspective of achieving success at home as a partner and/or parent, it is quite important to have a 100% commitment to doing the best you can.

I am fully committed to being the best I can be in my work and as a father and partner. My commitment to success provides me with the drive, determination and focus to do whatever it takes, to put up with whatever hardships and frustrations arise, to make my dream a reality – as much as humanly possible.

Never, ever give up:
The story of infomercial success and failure

I have always wanted to teach young people the tools they need to be successful and happy. I started this journey with the writing of my book with Darko Hajzler, *You Can Do It! What Every Student (and Parent) Should Know About Success in School and Life* (it became a best-seller!). In the book, we discussed the steps students could take to be successful and happy including: goal setting, time management, attitudes, self-confidence, self-acceptance, general study techniques, self-motivation, exam techniques and relationships.

Following the success of this book, including the positive impact it was having on young people, Patricia my creative business partner and wife, and I decided to see if we could produce an educational video program where all students could learn the tools for success and happiness. Our idea was that if we could also produce a 30-minute Infomercial that would appear on cable TV networks, we could bring this video program directly to students. As parents ourselves, we thought many parents would also be interested in what the program had to offer and would purchase the program for their children.

We knew this would be very risky in terms of finances, our time, and the track record of Infomercials with only 1 in 10 being successful.

We decided to be all in. So, this is what we set about doing.

We raised some investor finance for the production of the You Can Do It! Education video for students and for a 30-minute Infomercial. We worked with script writers, a production company and hired a TV star, Susan Dey, who was starring in *LA Law* (and won a Golden Globe), to appear in the Infomercial.

Michael Bernard celebrates with Susan Dey

From start to finish, it took us 12 months of 24/7 work.

And we succeeded in producing a first-class+ educational video program for students and a 30-minute Infomercial.

Marketing the program in magazines and showing the Infomercial on cable TV was our next challenge.

At this stage, we learnt a very important lesson about having a Commitment to Success – it does not guarantee success. We dreamt big, very big. We worked harder than ever, learnt so much about a new industry and put up with incredible stress and strain of keeping to a timeline and budget. And we believe we delivered in spades!

The bad news was that for different reasons and factors we couldn't control, we were unable to generate a sufficiently positive response of parents accessing the program for their children to sustain continued efforts to market. We received great feedback on the quality of our work and we did manage to sell programs, just not enough.

After 18 months, we gave up on the idea that our educational program and Infomercial could be a great vehicle for reaching the minds of lots of students.

I wouldn't be honest if I said it didn't effect our morale and wellbeing. First, we took some time out from development and focused on staying positive and spending time enjoying our two kids during their school years in Laguna Beach, California, where we had the opportunity to be closely connected with their great schools and the committed parenting community before we returned back home to Australia where our hearts still belonged and where our program was needed.

Fast forward to today where over the past two decades, in Australia and overseas, over 1,000,000 students have participated in You Can Do It! Education programs at their schools (3-year-olds to 18-year-olds) and now we are working with university students. We experimented in program development becoming one of the first online digital curricula programs of its kind worldwide.

And the road to success of many or our friends who are extremely successful in their work is littered with similar stories of failure. However, due to their Commitment to Success, they re-started their journey, maintaining the self-belief, determination and focus to go one better.

How committed are you to success? How strong are your beliefs?

The way to tell or judge your Commitment to Success is by the extent to which you put into practice as often and effectively as possible at work, home and life five success-oriented beliefs: Self-direction, Optimism, Growth Mindset, High Frustration Tolerance and Creativity.

To aid your self-awareness, you can complete the survey that appears on the next page: *Survey of the High Performance Mindset. Commitment to Success.*

Complete this survey online:

DISCOVER YOUR LEVEL OF MINDSET STRENGTH – TAKE THE HIGH PERFORMANCE MINDSET AT WORK SURVEY

youcandoiteducation.com.au/2017/10/30/high-performance-mindset-at-work-survey/

Before you get started, here's a guide for interpreting your total score for beliefs that support your Commitment to Success.

Total Score: 12 – 14 – a strongly held belief you put into practice on a regular basis
Total Score: 8 – 10 – a belief that needs to more regularly be put into practice
Total Score: 2 – 6 – you do not endorse the belief and/or put it into practice

Your scores on the survey may highlight beliefs that may not be as strong as they need to be. However, you will be the best judge of whether or not you need to further develop one or more of the five success-oriented beliefs.

The pages which follow the survey will provide you with lots of ideas and tips for strengthening one or all of the success-oriented beliefs.

One final point. Without these beliefs being a part of my mind – deeply embedded in my inner CEO, my pre-frontal cortex, I would be struggling and drowning today. The good news is that by becoming aware of these beliefs and putting them into action at work, home and life, you will feel more in control of your destiny.

SURVEY OF THE HIGH PERFORMANCE MINDSET: COMMITMENT TO SUCCESS

Instructions: Please indicate how often you put the following beliefs into practice at work, home and life.

		Never	Rarely	Some times	Not Sure	Often	Almost Always	Always	Your Score
Self-Direction									
1	I believe in the importance of formulating specific short- and long-term goals about what I want to learn and achieve.	1	2	3	4	5	6	7	
2	When faced with difficult people and circumstances, I believe it is vital to put in sustained effort to overcome obstacles rather than being distracted and focusing too much on the negative.	1	2	3	4	5	6	7	
Optimism									
3	When I begin work on a project or task, I trust that I am much more likely to be successful than to fail.	1	2	3	4	5	6	7	
4	When I have had a setback in something I set out to accomplish, I see as temporary and that I am still likely to achieve good results in other things I am doing.	1	2	3	4	5	6	7	
Growth Mindset									
5	I believe that my competence and abilities always grow through effort, learning and experience.	1	2	3	4	5	6	7	
6	I believe I become smarter as I try harder and challenge myself to try different things to solve problems.	1	2	3	4	5	6	7	
High Frustration Tolerance									
7	I know that tolerance of frustration and the sacrifice of fun things is often necessary to be successful in the long-term.	1	2	3	4	5	6	7	
8	I believe that I have enough 'willpower' to overcome times when feel bored and un-motivated.	1	2	3	4	5	6	7	
Creativity									
9	When faced with challenges and obstacles at work, I am very open to sharing my creative ideas with others.	1	2	3	4	5	6	7	
10	I have a very free and open approach to considering problems and I believe in the importance of exploring "outside of the box" solutions.	1	2	3	4	5	6	7	

ADD SCORES FOR TOTAL COMMITMENT TO SUCCESS

Place an asterix (*) next to the beliefs you need to more consistently put into practice to increase your Commitment to Success.

COMMITMENT TO SUCCESS

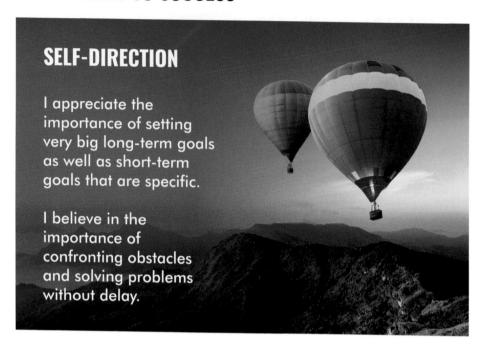

SELF-DIRECTION

I appreciate the importance of setting very big long-term goals as well as short-term goals that are specific.

I believe in the importance of confronting obstacles and solving problems without delay.

Tips for strengthening self-direction

Imagine your long-term goals (3 – 5 years+). Don't be afraid to set them very high.

Focus on your concrete short-term goals (3 – 6 months).

At the beginning of a day or week, be specific in writing down what you want to accomplish (and when you are going to do it).

When you do not at first achieve your goal, remember it takes time to re-train your brain and that with practice, your ability to achieve goals will improve.

Setting goals just to please others is not as good as deciding for yourself what you want to do.

Make sure to write down your goal (specific details, realistic) and review the goal on a regular basis.

Face problems squarely on. Whether it is a difficult colleague or piles of work to do, figure out different ways to immediately solve the problem.

COMMITMENT TO SUCCESS

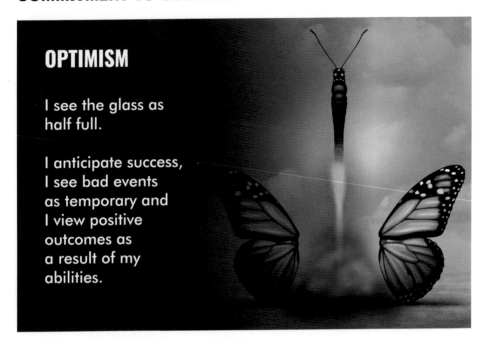

OPTIMISM

I see the glass as half full.

I anticipate success, I see bad events as temporary and I view positive outcomes as a result of my abilities.

Tips for strengthening optimism

Review the things you have achieved in the past that were extremely challenging and difficult.

Remind yourself you have done hard things before, therefore you can be successful in tackling the next challenge and problem.

After you have accomplished a challenging task or project, take credit (e.g., "I have the talent and skill to be successful.").

When you have not been successful, do not explain the failure in terms of you not having talent. Rather, search for the "real" reasons such as lack of 100% effort or competing demands.

Search for partial rather than perfect solutions.

When faced with a challenging task, situation or person, play a mental video of yourself achieving a preferred outcome.

When faced with a setback: 1. See it as temporary rather than permanent, 2. See it as specific to the job you were working on – rather than a sign of likely setbacks in all areas of work, and 3. Rather than taking full blame for the setback, explore other reasons that might have led to the setback.

Avoid pessimistic people and as much as possible surround yourself with positive people at work, home and life.

COMMITMENT TO SUCCESS

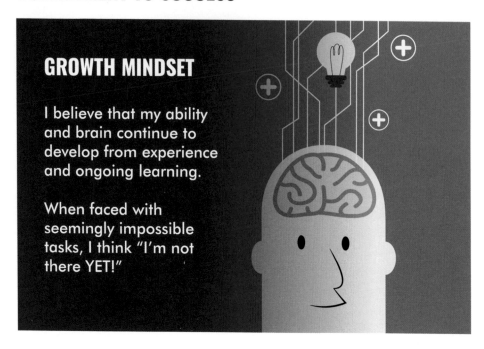

GROWTH MINDSET

I believe that my ability and brain continue to develop from experience and ongoing learning.

When faced with seemingly impossible tasks, I think "I'm not there YET!"

Tips for strengthening a growth mindset

If you catch yourself saying "I can't do that" – just add the word "YET" to the end of the sentence.

Appreciate that your effort is the key to new learning and advancement.

See what you can learn from the successes of others.

Take stock of what you have learned from previous successes and failures.

When you notice that nothing seems to change and you are facing the same problems and challenges, ask yourself "What can I learn from this situation to do things differently?"

See what you can learn from the criticisms of others, find out what they are really saying.

When you make mistakes or fail at a task, make a conscious effort to learn what you can about what went wrong or what you could do differently next time.

Enrol in programs and classes that further your knowledge and skill-set (technical and EQ).

Exercise your brain – it's like a muscle, it strengthens with constant use and exertion.

COMMITMENT TO SUCCESS

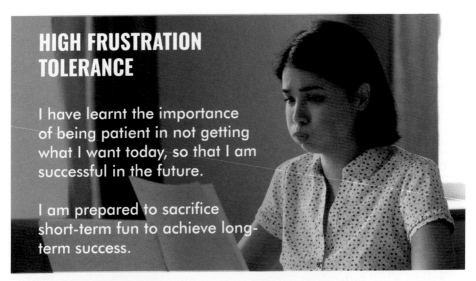

HIGH FRUSTRATION TOLERANCE

I have learnt the importance of being patient in not getting what I want today, so that I am successful in the future.

I am prepared to sacrifice short-term fun to achieve long-term success.

Tips for strengthening high frustration tolerance

Make a list of all the advantages of putting up with highly frustrating tasks and people and a list of all the disadvantages of task and people avoidance; review the list regularly.

Convince yourself on a regular basis that in order to achieve pleasant results in the long-term, you sometimes have to put up with highly frustrating tasks and people in the short-term.

Design your work and home environments so that you do not allow frustrating tasks to accumulate; do not let work pile up.

To increase your tolerance for frustration, ask yourself when life pulls a fast one on you: 'Is it true that I can't stand this situation or is it truer that I don't like this situation?'

Strengthen your body to buffer the stress effects of multiple frustrations through maintaining a consistent, moderate, physical exercise program, healthy diet, and by getting adequate sleep.

Remind yourself you are the captain of your own ship; you control your destiny by the decisions you make.

Make a list of the everyday situations that annoy you (driving on the highway at rush hour, waiting on hold for a customer service representative, etc.) and expose yourself to them gradually so that you can increase your tolerance.

Re-tool your perspective. As an example, ask yourself: "Of all the upsetting things that have happened to me in my life, getting criticised by my boss in front of my client was a 7 on a scale of 1 to 10, but not getting a seat on the subway this morning only gets a 2."

COMMITMENT TO SUCCESS

CREATIVITY

I believe in the importance of generating new, different solutions, ideas, or possibilities that may be useful in solving problems.

Tips for strengthening creativity

Take time out of your hectic schedule to daydream.

Suspend judgment while brainstorming ways to go about achieving the best results including getting out of situations you are in.

Commit yourself to taking an online learning course on the subject of creativity.

Get up early or stay up late. It's important to find your ideal creative time and stick to it. Pick the hours when your energy is high and distractions are minimal and give your creative work undivided attention for that block of time.

Go solo. Carve out some time to commune with your thoughts without other voices getting in the way.

Do something physical. Research has shown that physical exercise helps to force you out of left brain dominant thinking and instead adopt a more creative mindset.

Go solo. Carve out some time to commune with your thoughts without other voices getting in the way.

Embrace boredom. Research shows that being bored actually propels us towards deeper thinking and creativity.

Your Commitment to Success: 10 key questions

1. Are you deep down fully committed to achieving your personal best – at work, home and beyond?

2. What does being extremely successful for you really look like in different areas of your life?

3. Are you afraid to fail?

4. Does your modesty and humility get in the way of doing what it takes to reach the top of your mountains?

5. At your age, do you think that you've peaked in terms of what you are capable of achieving in different areas of your life?

6. Do you think it's really unfair that you have to work so hard to achieve great success when others seem to have it much easier?

7. Do you surround yourself with people who are achieving great results at work, home and life?

8. What are the small steps you can take today to maximise what you want from life?

9. Which of your strengths of character (creativity, teamwork, love of learning) can you use more often to increase your success?

10. Do you take for granted what you have achieved so far in different areas of your life?

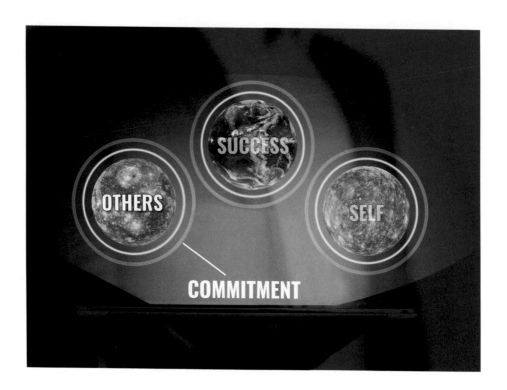

"No one is useless in this world who lightens the burdens of another."
Charles Dickens, author, *Doctor Marigold*

"I don't want to live in the kind of world where we don't look out for each other. Not just the people that are close to us, but anybody who needs a helping hand. I can't change the way anybody else thinks, or what they choose to do, but I can do my bit."
Charles de Lint, author, *Moonheart*

"No one has ever become poor by giving."
Anne Frank, *Diary of Anne Frank*

"We only have what we give."
Isabel Allende, author, *The Long Petal of the Sea*

"Doing nothing for others is the undoing of ourselves."
Horace Mann, educator

A Commitment to Others means that you have a strong desire and dedication to support and help others to grow, learn and advance without expecting anything back in return.

A Commitment to Others is an essential ingredient for not only forming but keeping relationships together.

The extent of your Commitment to Others has a big influence on your wellbeing and effectiveness in all areas of your life – and in the different roles you play. Some researchers have found that the greatest predictor of success and happiness is social support – the amount you give, rather than the amount you receive.

7 scientific benefits of helping others

(https://www.mentalfloss.com/article/71964/7-scientific-benefits-helping-others)

1. Helping others can help you live longer

Think about regularly assisting at a soup kitchen or coaching a basketball team at an at-risk high school. Research has shown that these kinds of activities can improve health in ways that can length your lifespan – volunteers show an improved ability to manage stress and stave off disease as well as reduced rates of depression and an increased sense of life satisfaction – when they were performed on a regular basis.

2. Altruism is contagious

When one person performs a good deed, it causes a chain reaction of other altruistic acts. One study found that people are more likely to perform feats of generosity after observing another do the same. This effect can ripple throughout the community, inspiring dozens of individuals to make a difference.

3. Helping others makes us happy

One team of sociologists tracked 2000 people over a five-year period and found that Americans who described themselves as "very happy" volunteered at least 5.8 hours per month.

4. Helping others may help with chronic pain

According to one study, people who suffered from chronic pain tried working as peer volunteers. As a result, they experienced a reduction in their own symptoms.

5. Helping others lowers blood pressure

If you're at risk for heart problems, your doctor has probably told you to cut back on red meat or the hours at your stressful job. However, you should also consider adding something to your routine: a regular volunteer schedule. One piece of research showed that older individuals who volunteered for at least 200 hours a year decreased their risk of hypertension by a whopping 40 per cent.

6. Helping others promotes positive behaviours in teens

According to sociologists, teenagers who volunteer have better grades and self-image.

7. Helping others gives us a sense of purpose and satisfaction

Looking for more meaning in your day-to-day existence? Studies show that volunteering enhances an individual's overall sense of purpose and identity – particularly if they no longer hold a life-defining role like "worker" or "parent".

Additionally, in wanting to influence the behaviour of those you live with like your partner or kids as well as those at work who you lead or collaborate with, warm, caring relationships will motivate others to be willing to change their behaviour you have requested or suggested.

Some people are natural in establishing connections with others including making friends, establishing networks of support and expressing understanding and sympathy during times of need.

For some, the Commitment to Others evolves more slowly as responsibilities grow. And for some people, reaching out to others and providing unconditional love and support remains a work in progress.

People in the helping, social occupations such as teachers, nurses, counsellors and social workers often have stronger commitments to others than they do to their own success.

It is true that many people in their work have achieved great things because of their single-minded, strong determination and focus to succeed. The issue for these people is that when – because of their achievements – they get promoted to positions of leadership where they have responsibility for the performance and wellbeing of others, some do not rise to the occasion. The case study of Jimmy Chan illustrates this point.

Additionally, in order for family relationships to bloom and sustain themselves over the long-term, members of the family unit need to display high levels of understanding, reciprocity and caring.

Here's what I have learnt. As an only child, somewhat reticent by nature, I have been, in terms of my work, largely self-reliant in terms of formulating and conducting plans for the goals we want to achieve in the future. The exception to this is my partner who provides me with advice, direction and acts as a sounding board and the voice of realism I need.

On the home front, as a parent (and partner), I have been much more into my relationships than in other areas of my life – I ALWAYS stay close to my children and wife, and am willingly available to listen, show empathy, support, am respectful and provide feedback when called for.

Now, in the rest of my life, my social connectedness is not as strong as it could be – and I find that as a consequence, my sense of wellbeing can suffer. The more I reach out and connect, the happier I am.

I also find that being somewhat of a workaholic, when for sustained periods of time I have much to accomplish and not enough time, I can withdraw into myself, losing out on the opportunities to support and care about others.

The person closest to me that exemplifies a strong Commitment to Others is my son, Jonathon. Here's how he explains his mindset towards others.

Jonathon Bernard, Commitment to Others

Several years ago I got pretty sick. During my recovery period, I was taken out on a picnic by a co-worker. It was a great day and I felt so great for her efforts in reaching out to me. She wasn't expecting anything back in return – just was hoping that I would enjoy myself and get myself right.

I took away from that experience what I had always really known about myself and that I had it in my power to help others who needed a lift. I could see that you don't have to have a powerful role or be financially well off to enrich the life of others in small (or big ways).

Since then, on my radar screen is a commitment to do things for others – and not having to get anything tangible back in return.

I've been fortunate to have worked with a very dedicated group of people delivering meals to those in need for St. Vincent de Paul. During the week, I volunteer at my work to lead physical training sessions for those interested. And I keep an eye out for and lend a hand to people who I know who are doing it hard either on the relationship front or who are simply battling to keep up with their multiple responsibilities.

My Commitment to Others is two-fold: first, to enrich the life of someone else by sharing my time and, second, following through on what I set out to do, not wanting to let me or them down. I love to invest myself in others – 100 per cent in, warts and all. I think a Commitment to Others means you are not just sometimes there for someone, but you are always there when needed. Also, you allow people to see your vulnerability, their vulnerability, what makes you stressed, what makes them stressed. Sure you enjoy the highs of life together, but that's the easy half.

The glue, the moments that keep you connected, the times when you feel the support of your team, those are generally experienced when the sky is dark, the problems are big and the solution isn't clear.

Because you generally learn in these moments, I continuously learn more about myself - especially from people I am closest with.

Sometimes, I don't see the energy I invest in someone as selfless. I think it's selfish because of how much I get from the experience. When I invest, I generally reap a return. It could be instant or it could come down the track.

The bonus for me, my happiest moments, in reaching out to others is when I receive the return of my Commitment to Others. It's not that I am asking for it. It just happens.

It's because I feel honoured that someone is connecting with me. Taking emotional and physical time and putting it towards me.

Time is one of the most valuable things we have. To donate it to someone else is the greatest gift of all.

So, you can begin your exploration of your Commitment to Others by self-examining the extent to which you put into practice in all areas of your life, five beliefs.

Before you get started, here's a guide for interpreting your total score for beliefs that support your Commitment to Others.

Total Score: 12 – 14 – a strongly held belief you put into practice on a regular basis
Total Score: 8 – 10 – a belief that needs to more regularly be put into practice
Total Score: 2 – 6 – you do not endorse the belief and/or put it into practice

Your scores on the survey suggest beliefs that may not be as strong as they need to be. However, you will be the best judge of whether or not you need to further develop one or more of the five other-oriented beliefs.

The pages which follow the survey will provide you with lots of ideas and tips for strengthening one or all of the other-oriented beliefs.

SURVEY OF THE HIGH PERFORMANCE MINDSET: COMMITMENT TO OTHERS

Instructions: Please indicate how often you put the following beliefs into practice at work, home and life.

		Never	Rarely	Some times	Not Sure	Often	Almost Always	Always	Your Score
Acceptance of Others									
1	I avoid judging people too harshly when they do the wrong thing.	1	2	3	4	5	6	7	
2	While I prefer people to behave considerately and fairly and treat me well, I know that they don't have to and can accept it when they don't.	1	2	3	4	5	6	7	
Empathy									
3	I know the importance of understanding what someone else is feeling.	1	2	3	4	5	6	7	
4	When someone disagrees with me or I disagree with what he/she is saying, it is important to understand his/her point of view before I offer my opinion.	1	2	3	4	5	6	7	
Respect									
5	I know the importance of treating others with consideration and regard, especially those people I find difficult to get along with.	1	2	3	4	5	6	7	
6	I respect people even when I am critical of their opinions and actions. I recognise they have positive qualities and hidden potential.	1	2	3	4	5	6	7	
Support									
7	I know that the more I help people achieve their goals, the more likely it is that I will achieve my goals.	1	2	3	4	5	6	7	
8	I believe in the importance of giving consistent and genuine praise for the positive efforts and achievements of others, even to those who I don't get along with.	1	2	3	4	5	6	7	
Feedback									
9	I understand for people to learn and develop positive traits they need to receive feedback concerning their performance and behaviour.	1	2	3	4	5	6	7	
10	I believe in the importance of giving and receiving constructive positive and negative feedback.	1	2	3	4	5	6	7	

ADD SCORES FOR TOTAL COMMITMENT TO OTHERS
Place an asterix (*) next to the beliefs you need to more consistently put into practice to increase your Commitment to Others.

COMMITMENT TO OTHERS

ACCEPTANCE OF OTHERS

I accept that people are imperfect and sometimes behave unfairly or inconsiderately.

I do not judge people too harshly when they do the wrong thing.

Tips for strengthening acceptance of others

Acceptance of others is the ability to see that others have a right to be their own unique persons. That means having a right to their own feelings, thoughts and opinions. When you accept people for who they are, you let go of your desire to change them.

The point of everybody else's life is not to make you happy. What would your relationships be like if you accepted the people around you exactly as they are?

Don't judge people for not being like you.

Pay more attention to your thoughts and do your best to push them in a non-judgmental, more accepting direction.

Ask yourself: What if someone were judging me and not accepting me? How would I feel?

In considering a person whose behaviour is disagreeable or obnoxious, try to discover their positive characteristics and do not judge people by their behaviour.

When faced with a person whose behaviour you find difficult (negative, disrespectful, unfair), dispute with yourself the idea that the person is totally bad and deserves retaliation for their behaviour.

Accept that people who do the wrong thing are not totally bad people in all respects and that people have the right to be wrong.

Persuade yourself that you can work with people whose behaviour you find disagreeable.

Remind yourself that you have until now lived with and tolerated bad behaviour of others and that you can continue to do so.

COMMITMENT TO OTHERS

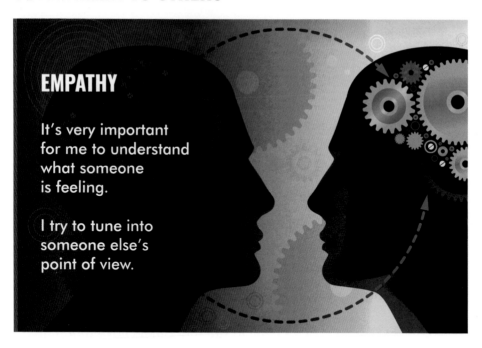

EMPATHY

It's very important for me to understand what someone is feeling.

I try to tune into someone else's point of view.

Tips for strengthening empathy

Consider the notion that the measure of empathy is how you treat someone who is of absolutely no use to you. Empathy should not be selective.

A useful focus to aim for when listening to another person is to try to understand how the other person feels, and to discover what they want to achieve.

Establishing trust is about listening and understanding – not necessarily agreeing (which is different) – to the other person.

Listen without judging.

Practice not interrupting people. Do not dismiss their concerns offhand. Do not rush to give advice. Do not change the subject. Allow people their moment.

Consider that it is difficult and rarely appropriate to try to persuade another person to do what you want; instead you must understand what the other person wants, and then try help them to achieve it, which often includes helping them to see the way to do it.

Listening does not come naturally to most people, so you may need to work hard at it; stop yourself from "jumping in" and giving your opinions, see and feel the situation from the other person's position.

COMMITMENT TO OTHERS

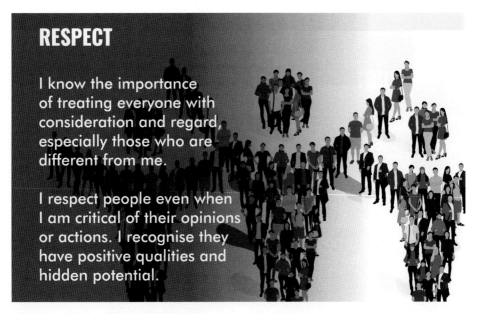

RESPECT

I know the importance of treating everyone with consideration and regard, especially those who are different from me.

I respect people even when I am critical of their opinions or actions. I recognise they have positive qualities and hidden potential.

Tips for strengthening respect

Be fully present when you are with people. Don't check your email, look at your watch or take phone calls when someone drops by to talk to you. Put yourself in their shoes. How would you feel if they did that to you?

Keep your promise. By keeping your word to someone, you not only establish yourself as a person of integrity, but make the other person feel as though you value them.

Be on time. Another way to demonstrate that you value someone – is by treating his or her time as though it is valuable. Nothing says this better than being punctual.

Go out of your way. You don't have to always do the bare minimum. If you want to show someone that they're valuable, and that you respect them, go the extra mile without expecting a reward.

Don't force your opinion on others.

Be mindful of the Golden Rule, "Do unto others as you would have them do unto you".

Use people's name. Also remember the names of people's spouse and children so that you can refer to them by name.

Take a personal interest in people. Show people that you care and are genuinely curious about their lives. Ask them questions about their hobbies, their challenges, their families, and their aspirations.

COMMITMENT TO OTHERS

SUPPORT

I value doing things for others.

I focus on how I can increase the amount of social support I provide people in my life.

Tips for strengthening support

Go out of your way to understand ways in which you can help others to achieve their goals.

Volunteer to do small things for others to help them get things done.

Take a moment out of your day to ask, "How are things going?"

Remind yourself on a regular basis that the more you help others to be successful, the more you will be successful.

Be available to listen and offer advice for someone who is faced with a problem that is causing stress.

When you hear a silly idea, do not shoot someone down and make him or her feel unimportant. Instead, genuinely encourage them.

Encourage people, particularly the quiet ones, to speak up. A simple thing like an attentive nod can boost people's confidence.

Offer your help and offer specific ways that you would like to help.

Give time, energy, resources… give yourself. Just don't give advice when they haven't asked.

Listen. Let them be honest when life is hard. Let them be angry. Let them be whatever they need to be, and resist the urge to fix them, heal them, or placate them. Just be with them.

COMMITMENT TO OTHERS

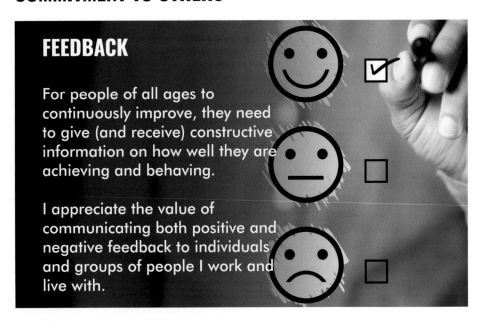

FEEDBACK

For people of all ages to continuously improve, they need to give (and receive) constructive information on how well they are achieving and behaving.

I appreciate the value of communicating both positive and negative feedback to individuals and groups of people I work and live with.

Tips for strengthening feedback

Focus on what the person is doing well when giving feedback (and not just what they can improve upon).

Provide tangible examples of the behaviour in question, not vague, "drive by" criticism like, "You've been arguing a lot."

The closer feedback is tied to the behaviour in question (good or bad) the more powerful it will be.

Take time to engage with the person to check for understanding. Focus on "partnership", not "this is what you're doing wrong" or "this is what you need to change".

When you provide constructive, negative feedback to another on their opinion or how they are doing an aspect of their job, do so in a calm manner making sure that you do not make the person feel you are putting them down.

At a suitable time, discuss with others the idea that it is important not to take negative feedback personally and that disagreeing with another's opinion or being critical of aspects of their work performance is not a sign of disrespect.

Give genuine recognition and praise. Pay attention to what people are doing and catch them doing the right things. When you give praise, spend a little effort to make your genuine words memorable: "You are an asset to this team because..."; "This was pure genius"; "I would have missed this if you hadn't picked it up."

Your Commitment to Others: 10 key questions

1. Do you disagree agreeably?

2. Do you compromise?

3. Do you need to prove you are always right?

4. Do you take time to truly listen?

5. Are you interested in promoting the growth of others?

6. Do you wait for people to contact you?

7. Are you comfortable asking someone if they would like your help?

8. Do you withhold compliments or help for someone who has done the wrong thing by you?

9. Do you find it difficult to offer praise?

10. Do you prefer to work alone or in a group?

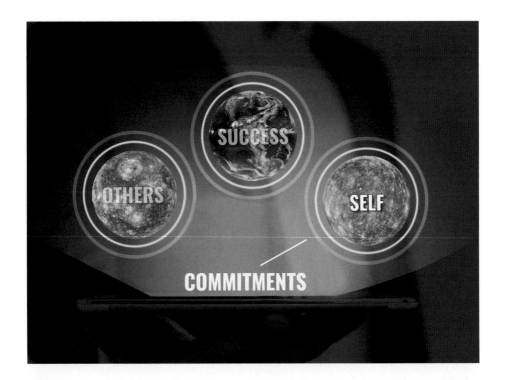

"It is health that is real wealth and not pieces of gold and silver."
Gandhi, leader of India's non-violent independence movement

"Healthy and happy people accept themselves because they are
alive and have some capacity to enjoy themselves. They refuse
to measure their intrinsic worth by their extrinsic achievement or
what others think of them. They frankly chose to accept themselves
unconditionally; and they try to completely avoid rating themselves."
Albert Ellis, founder Rational Emotive, Cognitive Behavior Therapy

"Let us be grateful to people who make us happy, they are
the charming gardeners who make our souls blossom."
Marcel Proust, novelist, *In Search of Lost Time*

"Successful people maintain a positive focus in life no matter
what's going on around them."
Jack Canfield, author, *Chicken Soup for the Soul*

PERSONAL RESPONSIBILITY FOR SELF

It is surprising that for many people, Commitment to Self is not the strongest of the three commitments. Why do you think this is so?

The stress of modern-day living can interfere. Also, a Commitment to Self involves mental health and wellbeing issues that can make it harder for people to know how to protect and enhance their sense of self.

Personal responsibility for self

Recently, I was presenting a talk on stress management at Positive Schools Conferences across Australia. During the presentation, I described actions schools could take to reduce stressful working conditions. I also illustrated how people can develop healthy attitudes and coping skills to assist them to self-manage levels of stress – to great effect! I mentioned that over 20 years ago, I began strengthening my own resilience and if I hadn't, I would have been "stuffed", much less able to overcome the muddles and puddles of life. Now, in the final question/answer part of the program, I was asked: "You said you started to learn about how to manage stress. What started you on this journey?" I had to pause and reflect and then I replied: "I read the writing on the wall. I realised that no one I worked for and no one at home was going to look after me and rescue me from stress. I realised I had to start to look after myself. And so I have – getting smarter as the years roll on – I hope!"

Twenty years ago, I made a conscious decision to strengthen my Commitment to Self – so that today I take actions to maintain a positive sense of who I am.

Without strong Commitment to Self, people find it much harder to be loved and accepted by others, to achieve their personal best at work, to be relatively stress-free, to be happy and to live a long life.

The Commitment to Self trio

One aspect of Commitment to Self is focussed on **physical** health. Here, you make a solemn, unbreakable promise to yourself to exercise on a regular basis, eat a balanced, healthy diet based on your nutritional needs and limit your caloric intake so that you maintain your ideal body weight.

A second aspect of your Commitment to Self concerns your **social** involvements. Here, you recognise that your happiness is often (but not always) enhanced through the give and take of friendships. You make sure on a regular basis that you are nurturing existing relationships with family, friends and colleagues and when necessary extend your circle of friends. You put the time and effort into relationships knowing this investment helps build a strong family, circle of friends, effective teams and community.

The third aspect of Commitment to Self concerns your **emotional** wellbeing. Here, you make a conscious decision to take charge of you. As a priority, you take steps to protect your self against harmful negative thinking, feeling and behaviour. Rather than spending all of your time meeting the needs of others, you make a point of spending some of your time doing things you find interesting and enjoyable.

My daughter, Alex, is a very giving and loving person to family and friends – she is unselfish. Yet, she has developed an awareness that she needs to make a commitment to herself – and so she has!

Alexandra Bernard, Commitment to Self

Eight years ago I moved to a small town in the US to support my partner while he pursued his interest of getting a MBA degree. We packed up our home and moved across the world, leaving our closest family and friends behind. We moved to a small college town in upstate NY where we knew no one. My partner was soon preoccupied with his new studies and post-graduate classmates. During this time, I was determined to forge a life for my own. So, I decided to make a commitment to myself. Actually, multiple commitments to myself. I did not blame my partner for moving to such a remote place. This commitment to myself didn't mean I wanted or needed to be selfish – not at all. I just knew that there was no one really able to look after me, but me.

I realised that I needed to socialise with new friends. I actively set out to find opportunities to attend social activities – and I avoided designing my daily life around my work which was somewhat solitary as a researcher.

I knew that for me to deal with the strain of being away from home and living in an unfamiliar place, I needed to become even more strongly determined to be physically fit. Part of my commitment to my physical self involved and continues to be eating properly and exercise.

I also made a commitment to myself that I wanted to be happy in my new surroundings. I made a conscious decision to be positive within myself. I knew this was important for my partner and for me, emotionally. A lot of this involved me focussing on and being grateful for the positives I had in my life. I took each day as it came and immersed myself in making the most of my new situation.

I explored my new surroundings. I enjoyed new hobbies. Based on the supplies I could find, I decorated our home, I found new workouts expanding my experience of hiking on trails, picked up arts and crafts, practiced mindfulness as part of my regular routine.

Each day I set mini goals – make a new recipe, walk a new trail, speak to a new person, write to someone back home. This meant I had something I was proud of at the end of each day.

Looking back at my time in upstate NY – it was hard. Living away from friends and family, in a new place, in extreme weather, without my own identity – I would be lying if I didn't say it was hard. But whilst some people would want to erase that time period from their memories, I'm proud of getting through it. I'm proud of what I accomplished for me during that time.

So, you can begin your exploration of your Commitment to Self by self-examining the extent to which you put into practice in all areas of your life, five beliefs.

Before you get started, here's a guide for interpreting your total score for beliefs that support your Commitment to Self.

Total Score: 12 – 14 – a strongly held belief you put into practice on a regular basis
Total Score: 8 – 10 – a belief that needs to more regularly be put into practice
Total Score: 2 – 6 – you do not endorse the belief and/or put it into practice

The pages which follow the survey will provide you with lots of ideas and tips for strengthening one or all of the beliefs concerning your self.

SURVEY OF THE HIGH PERFORMANCE MINDSET: COMMITMENT TO SELF

Instructions: Please indicate how often you put the following beliefs into practice at work, home and life.

		Never	Rarely	Some times	Not Sure	Often	Almost Always	Always	Your Score
Self-acceptance									
1	I appreciate that my worth as a person is separate from how others view me or how I perform at work and home.	1	2	3	4	5	6	7	
2	I realise the importance of not taking things personally.	1	2	3	4	5	6	7	
Positive Self-Regard									
3	I appreciate myself as a person.	1	2	3	4	5	6	7	
4	When things are not going well, I keep in mind my positive qualities.	1	2	3	4	5	6	7	
Positive focus									
5	It is important to be grateful for the good things that people do to help support me rather than what they do not do.	1	2	3	4	5	6	7	
6	It is important to focus on the good things that happen rather than the bad.	1	2	3	4	5	6	7	
Authenticity									
7	I am true to myself and stand up for what I believe in.	1	2	3	4	5	6	7	
8	What I say reflects my true beliefs about how I see things and what I believe is right.	1	2	3	4	5	6	7	
Healthy Living									
9	Exercise, rest and a good diet leads to a healthy mind and body.	1	2	3	4	5	6	7	
10	I consider it important for me to spend time with family and friends.	1	2	3	4	5	6	7	

ADD SCORES FOR TOTAL COMMITMENT TO SELF

Place an asterix (*) next to the beliefs you need to more consistently put into practice to increase your Commitment to Self.

COMMITMENT TO SELF

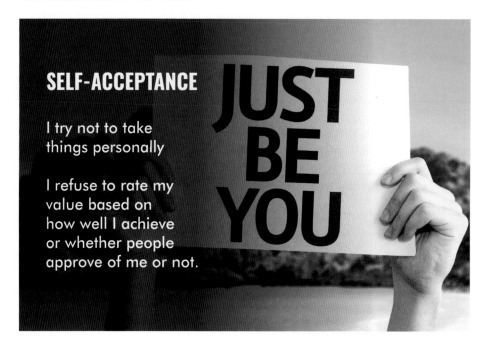

SELF-ACCEPTANCE

I try not to take things personally

I refuse to rate my value based on how well I achieve or whether people approve of me or not.

JUST BE YOU

Tips for strengthening self-acceptance

✓ Remind yourself that all human beings are fallible and will make mistakes from time to time. Work on accepting yourself with everything about you.

✓ When faced with sub-standard work performance/negative work evaluation or some form of rejection, remind yourself that your value as a person cannot be determined by your work performance or how others value you.

✓ Eliminate all forms of self-rating. You are never a great person, only a person who may do great things. And you are never a bad person for acting badly.

✓ Decide on a self-acceptance self-statement and repeat it every day (e.g., "I accept myself just as I am." "I accept myself no matter what" "I accept myself warts and all.").

✓ Get in the habit of not comparing yourself to others.

✓ Remind yourself that just as it never makes sense to trash a car because it has a flat tire, it never makes sense to trash yourself when things do not work out or others are critical of you.

COMMITMENT TO SELF

POSITIVE SELF-REGARD

I am proud of who I am.

I remind myself of my positive personal qualities.

Tips to strengthen positive self-regard

- ✓ Take stock of your character strengths (visit:www.authentichappiness.sas.upenn.edu/tests).
- ✓ Develop a full understanding and appreciation of your strengths of multiple intelligence (visual-spatial, body-kinesthetic, musical, interpersonal, intrapersonal, linguistic, logical-mathematical).
- ✓ Be mindful of those aspects of your family, cultural and religious background you are proud of.
- ✓ Identify and participate in activities that involve you using your talents and strengths.
- ✓ Focus as much as possible on your talents and positive aspects of who you are; avoid focusing on your negatives.
- ✓ Do not take your positive qualities for granted.

COMMITMENT TO SELF

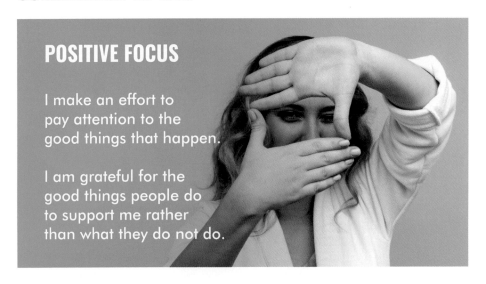

POSITIVE FOCUS

I make an effort to
pay attention to the
good things that happen.

I am grateful for the
good things people do
to support me rather
than what they do not do.

Tips for strengthening a positive focus

✓ Focus on the present and not on the negatives of the past.
✓ Each day when you wake up give yourself a mini pep-talk – what
   do you want to achieve? How will you react to trying situations?
   How will you avoid negative thoughts?
✓ Remember, thinking positive is a habit, which means it's possible
   to learn how to do it.
✓ Accept when things aren't perfect. It can be difficult to let go of
   the need for perfection and control in your life, but sometimes it's
   very liberating to simply accept that things will not always go the
   way you hoped, and that's okay. Sometimes things happen that
   are out of your control, and rather than wasting your energy on
   negative emotions, it's better to just accept that things didn't go
   the way you planned or wanted.
✓ The more frequently you spend time with positive thinking people,
   the more likely it is that you will begin to think and act in a similar
   fashion.
✓ Be grateful by spending a little time each day thinking of things
   that you are truly thankful for in your life.
✓ A good practice to get into is that of keeping a gratitude journal.
   This is where you make a note of 3-5 things that make you happy
   or thankful each day. This is one of the best ways to promote the
   habit of gratitude.

COMMITMENT TO SELF

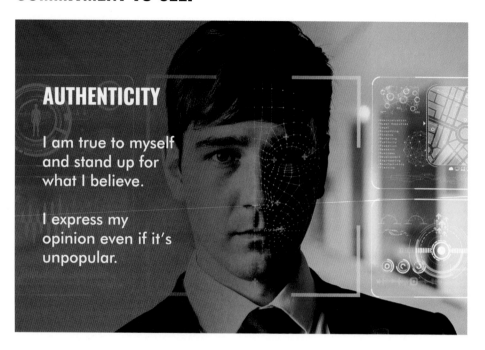

AUTHENTICITY

I am true to myself
and stand up for
what I believe.

I express my
opinion even if it's
unpopular.

Tips for strengthening authenticity

✓ Practice speaking from the heart and showing others what you
   truly believe in – and who you are.
✓ Make an effort to be interested in another person rather than
   trying to get another person interested in you.
✓ Do the right things even if it means loss of benefit to you.
✓ Honour and trust your intuition.
✓ Do not be afraid to say what you believe to be true.
✓ Know that the more you become aware of your true feelings
   about people and the way things are being done, the greater
   scope you have for personal growth.
✓ Do not hide behind the opinions of others and agree simply to
   agree. And do not put on a show merely to please others.
✓ Discard those beliefs you have that are not consistent with the
   type of person you want to be.

COMMITMENT TO SELF

HEALTHY LIVING

I am careful to exercise, relax and watch what I eat.

It is important to my wellbeing to spend time with friends.

Tips to strengthen healthy living

✓ Regularly remind yourself why you want to be healthy.
✓ Take responsibility for managing your health by scheduling regular physical check-ups.
✓ Consider the extent to which your diet conforms to principles of good health. Consult healthy eating guidelines to learn the appropriate balance of plant foods (vegetables, fruits, nuts, breads, cereals); fish, meat, chicken, eggs, cheese and yoghurt; foods with unhealthy amounts of sugar and fats.
✓ Do you need to increase water intake to between 6-8 glasses of water per day?
✓ Do you need to cut back on caffeine, sweets and alcohol?
✓ Schedule and engage in some form of exercise at least four times a week.
✓ If it suits you, join a group or see if someone you know is also interested in keeping fit.
✓ Try setting goals together.
✓ Relaxation is important. Relaxing and managing stress is an essential part of being healthy. Set aside time for ways to relax such as listening to music or slow breathing.
✓ It's natural at times to feel like giving up and going back to old habits. If you slip-up, be realistic and start again.

Your Commitment to Self: 10 key questions

1. Do you make time for yourself?

2. Do you take things personally?

3. When things are not going well and you hold yourself responsible, how good are you in maintaining a positive view of you and your positives?

4. Are you OK to express an opinion that is different from what the majority or your senior thinks?

5. What draws your attention, what is going right or what is going wrong?

6. Do you find it impossible to find time to exercise?

7. Do you mostly if not always put other people's needs before yours?

8. Do you spend enough time with friends?

9. Do you feel the need to prove yourself to others?

10. Are you someone who accepts him/herself despite your imperfections and fallibilities?

STRENGTHENING A COMMITMENT

To strengthen a commitment, you can take the following three steps:

1. Select one of the three commitments you want to strengthen (Success, Others, Self).
2. Select one or more of the beliefs that support the commitment that you need to put into practice more often.
3. Put the beliefs into practice at every opportunity.

Suppose you want to increase your Commitment to Self. From the *Survey of The High Performance Mindset: Commitment to Self*, you might have noticed that while you agree with most of the beliefs listed, you do not consistently act on them. For example, while you might agree with the importance of having a positive focus, you tend to dwell more on the negatives than the positives. If this is the case, you would take it upon yourself to keep track of the positive events you experience inside and outside of work and home and rather than taking them for granted, you begin to value them as being very important – even more important than the negative events you encounter.

By completing the *Strengthening Commitments Guide* that follows, you can begin the process of putting into practice those beliefs which are constituent elements of the high performance mindset. Now that you are aware of the three commitments at the foundation of a high performance mindset, you can decide whether or not there is much room for growth. You might have discovered that you are already committed to success, others and to your self – or you can more clearly see that one or all of the commitments can be further developed. In which case, you will have noted one or more beliefs that you could put into practice more often to strengthen a commitment.

The story of a high performance mindset continues now with an illumination of four internal blockers that can arise when you are confronted with very tough situations. These include challenging tasks, difficult people, work overload, organisational screw-ups, issues with our children, or disagreements with our partner. If you are not resilient enough to cope with these events then they can pull you downwards, sometimes so low that we can burn out or simply give up.

BUCKLE UP!

STRENGTHENING COMMITMENTS GUIDE

Instructions: Indicate the areas where your commitment needs to be increased:

☐ Commitment to Success

☐ Commitment to Others

☐ Commitment to Self

Which beliefs do you need to put into practice on a more regular basis (review at the beginning and end of each day):

	Start of Day	End of Day
Self-Direction	☐	☐
Acceptance of Others	☐	☐
Self-Acceptance	☐	☐
Optimism	☐	☐
Empathy	☐	☐
Positive Self-Regard	☐	☐
Growth	☐	☐
Respect	☐	☐
Authenticity	☐	☐
High Frustration Tolerance	☐	☐
Support	☐	☐
Positive Focus	☐	☐
Creativity	☐	☐
Feedback	☐	☐
Healthy Living	☐	☐

Describe the actions you will take to put one or more beliefs into practice:

_____

_____

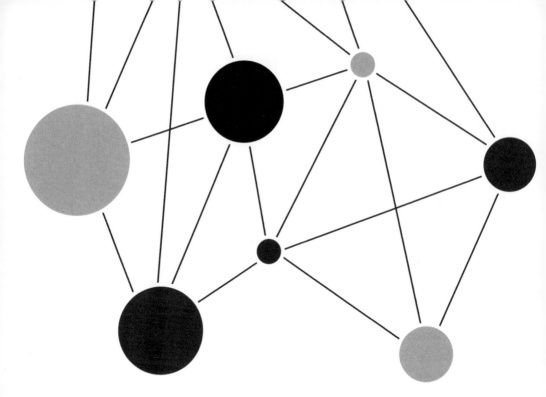

Part 3

Blockers

MEET THE BLOCKERS

With the three strong commitments discussed in Part 2 of this book, you will have the foundations needed to perform at your personal best and to experience a very high level of wellbeing at work, home and in other areas of life.

And normally you will have the forward momentum toward your goals that your commitments provide.

However, everyone no matter how strong their commitments encounter tough situations and difficult people that threaten their capacity to cope, manage, solve problems effectively and achieve goals.

At these times, people experience one or more of what I call blockers that lead to a downward spiral in their positivity, momentum and how well they perform.

The blockers that I am most interested in are the internal ones – those that occur within our minds that create confusion and loss of focus and determination.

CASE STUDY: THE 'BLOCKERS' OF JORDIE BLAKE

Several years ago, I worked with Jordie Blake (not his real name). Jordie, in his late 20's was from England and worked as a campaign developer for an advertising agency, Pure Concept, where he had been working for 18 months. Jordie was a talented developer of online advertising. Full of energy and addicted to the creative process, Jordie had initially impressed the company with his fresh ideas and technical knowledge for developing online content for brand building and web-based marketing.

At the time, he had a client allocation of two blue chip companies, and he prided himself on the strong relationships he had built with both clients.

Three months ago, before meeting with Jordie, Pure Concept underwent a business restructure and recruited two new senior managers including a new Account Manager, Agatha Johnson, who Jordie was to report to. As a result of these changes and the downturn in the economy (including less dollars being spent by existing clients on projects), the business direction shifted in emphasis from servicing existing clients to acquiring new ones, with all personnel now expected to participate in business development activities.

For Jordie this was not the greatest of news as he prefers to work with the creative team and he feels that his new manager was not appreciating his strongest skills set. He felt increasingly under the pump and was becoming more and more anxious as his perceived value seemed to be diminishing. His survival at Pure Concept depended not only on the creative-technical assistance he provides to his existing clients and other in-house projects, but also on how successful he was at generating new accounts.

Jordie's team has a routine meeting early on Monday mornings to deliver briefs on the progress of their campaigns. These meetings are usually informal and relatively light-hearted. Jordie is part of a close knit team that places a high value on not only having fun, but also getting the job done, which is why the team got quite a shock this particular Monday morning.

Jordie arrived at the meeting feeling flat and looking tense, angry and tired. He threw his file onto the table with only a cursory greeting to his team. He opened the meeting by telling everyone that "things are going to change around here" and proceeded to vent his anger about the e-mail he received from Agatha. He referred to the new manager as "a useless bean counter" who "clearly knows nothing about the value of the internet design in the process of establishing client branding" and talked about having been through this before in the UK when "developing new business became more important than servicing existing clients by adding value via the internet."

Jordie ended the meeting by telling his team that they "may as well go and get a job in PR rather than design" and walked out slamming the door behind him.

As soon as he is out of the room, Jordie realised that he has blown it by letting his team see his level of stress. This only adds to his high levels of anxiety about his performance at Pure Concept – how could they know he was tossing and turning all night knowing he has missed most of his new client targets for the last two months and the future wasn't looking good? To make matters worse, his new manager has scheduled a progress review meeting at the end of next week.

Initially consultative about the business direction and reasonably friendly, Agatha has recently become more formal in her communications with Jordie. She has sent him several requests for progress updates by email and yesterday while having a brief discussion with him in the staff lounge room, she even suggested that he "needs to buckle down and do some serious prioritising or else the business may not be able to carry you for that much longer."

Jordie returns to his office resigned to getting to work on sourcing some new clients. He knows that he has procrastinated about this aspect of his role and he doesn't know where to start. His desk is a disorganised mess, he does not have a strategy and when he checks his multiple missed deadlines he feels a sense of panic overwhelm him. "How dare she do this to me, doesn't she understand that I am a creative GENIUS? She doesn't value what I do and she thinks I am hopeless. Why should I waste my time on this crap?"

Jordie puts his head in his hands and thinks "What's the point – she's making it impossible for me to do my job effectively. I can't see how, with her around, I can do it. Maybe it's time to look for another job!" He turns his computer off and heads for the door.

To Jordie it feels just like the UK job he had to leave because he failed to build the business and consequently he and two of his colleagues were made redundant. He is terrified that he will be made redundant again and the horror of repeating this scenario has rendered him unable to sleep, unable to concentrate and he feels utterly inadequate: "What the hell is wrong with me, maybe I am hopeless, maybe she is right."

Jordie experienced all four of the more common internal blockers; namely, anxiety, feeling down, anger and procrastination. Their level of intensity posed a problem for him and the question was whether or not he was willing and able to make a shift with his mindset to reduce their disruptive influence. As you can read about at the end of Part 2, over a series of coaching sessions, Jordie strengthened his mindset to overcome blockers. The results were heartening.

Let's have a look at the four blockers that disrupt positive performance in tough situations and which contribute to high levels of stress at work and home.

The point to keep in mind is that it is quite normal and healthy to experience blockers especially when we are confronted with tough situations and difficult people. However, it's when these reactions become extreme that our performance suffers, and our commitments can be negatively effected. We can spend 70 or 80 per cent of our time focused on the problem rather than the solution.

ANXIETY

Anxiety is the state of engaging in chains of thoughts and images of a negative and uncontrollable nature in which mental and real attempts are made to avoid potential threats. We normally worry about the possibility and the consequences of three types of events occurring: 1. lack of success (perfection) 2. disapproval, criticism and/or rejection from those whose opinions and judgments matter, and 3. discomfort. (An example of worrying about being uncomfortable is when we ruminate about how uncomfortable we will be when attending a forthcoming function where we do not know anyone. At the same time, we might also worry about what people will think about us when we talk with them.)

Now, it is quite normal and regular to worry about upcoming situations where you might be not be as successful as you would prefer, where others might not rate you as positively as you would prefer and where you might have to endure higher levels of physiological discomfort than you would prefer.

However, when worry escalates to higher levels of anxiety and panic, we often experience negative effects such as not being able to think clearly, not being able to concentrate and undesirable levels of physiological arousal (sweaty palms, rapid heart rate, blushing, faintness, stammering voice) all of which can be not only extremely unpleasant but maladaptive. Extreme worry is almost always a blocker to positive work performance.

Self-Talk when worry is extreme: "I should always be successful in what I do. I need significant others to always approve of me and what I do. I need to be comfortable. It is awful and terrible to make mistakes, to be criticised and/or uncomfortable."

Goal: Moderate levels of worry and concern so that you remain focussed and confident in the face of forthcoming events that are challenges to your success and approval and are threats to your comfort.

FEELING DOWN

It is a fact of life that most people who hold high aspirations and expectations get down when they have failed to achieve their goals or when they have been negatively evaluated by others. Feeling down is not depression though extended periods of negative thoughts and feelings about one's self-worth can end up as depression.

It is remarkable that in the face of setbacks we can make life doubly difficult by adding on feelings of inadequacy as a result of what happens. When our performance at work or home is not at a standard we desire and when people are critical of what we say and do, we have a significant practical problem to solve so that, in the future, we achieve our goals.

However, feeling down about our state of affairs represents an additional emotional problem we have to solve as well. When we get down about practical problems at work, it is much harder to solve them. It is unfortunately the case that all of us to greater or lesser extents have tendencies to think irrationally about setbacks and rejections and it is our way of thinking that creates the emotional problem of feeling down about practical problems. Because of its impact on your self-belief and energy and the accompanying feelings of emptiness and hopelessness, feeling down is almost always a blocker to positive performance and blocks you from developing a high level Commitment to Self.

Self-Talk that leads to feeling down: "Because I have not been as successful as I need to be and/or because others are not thinking as highly of me as I need them to, this is a catastrophe, I cannot stand it. This shows how utterly worthless I really am. Not only am I hopeless in this area, I am hopeless at everything I do and this will always be the case."

Goal: Feeling only disappointed and sad, but still confident at those times when you have not performed well and/or have rightly been criticised for less than optimum performance.

ANGER

Anger is an emotion that often occurs in situations where unfairness, inconsideration, frustrating conditions or injustice is perceived. A colleague may have promised you he would accomplish something for you by a certain date and fails to deliver and you are forced to do it and carry your own load as well. Your husband expects you to do 95% of all housework. A senior executive fails to inform you in a timely fashion about changes that affect you. One of your children lies to you about an incident he was involved with at school. The list can be extensive.

Anger is frequently a misunderstood emotion in that it is viewed by the person who is angry as justifiable and normal. Some forms of anger are healthy, other forms are not. Healthy anger is an emotion of moderate intensity that helps people achieve their goals and which does not lead to negative consequences. Synonyms for healthy anger include irritation, displeasure, and annoyance. Synonyms for unhealthy anger include rage, hate and bitterness.

An important idea concerning anger is that when you are blocked from obtaining what you desire or when someone mistreats you, it is perfectly normal and appropriate to be moderately angry including being annoyed and irritated as such feelings will motivate you to take constructive action to see if you can make changes to a situation or to another person's behaviour. However, when you become extremely angry and hostile after being frustrated, it is quite likely that your aggressive behaviour will not only be unsuitable to rectify a situation, your behaviour will be viewed as provocative and will tend to exacerbate the situation.

Self-talk that creates your anger: "This person should treat me considerately, respectfully and fairly as I treat him. I can't stand to be treated this way. This person is a no-good so-and-so who deserves a good kick up the backside."

There are physiological consequences of angry self-talk and the resultant feelings of anger including, in the short-term, muscle tension, increased heart rate, stomach upset, and perceptual confusion and in the long-term, stomach ulcers, high blood pressure and heart attack.

Goal: Healthy, moderate levels of anger and assertion rather than rage and aggressive behaviour when faced with provocation.

PROCRASTINATION

Procrastination is naturally by definition a work performance blocker. Procrastination means that you deliberately delay doing something at work even though you see the disadvantages of the delay. You might put off doing tasks because they are boring, time consuming or tedious. You can put off doing things as a payback for someone treating you poorly. Or you can procrastinate at doing some tasks or trying something new because you are extremely worried about whether you will do it well enough. Procrastination becomes a significant blocker when you put off doing important things and, as a consequence, your positive performance suffers.

Self-Talk that leads to procrastination: "Things I do should always be fun and exciting. I shouldn't have to do things that are boring and tedious." "I'll do it tomorrow when I'm more in the mood." "I work best under pressure, so I'll wait until the deadline is tomorrow." "I can't stand doing tedious tasks." "I really do need to be relaxed and in the zone to do my best work."

Goal: When faced with tasks that need doing but which you find deathly dull and boring, do them first as efficiently as possible before moving on to things that you enjoy doing. Put off putting it off!

Now that you are familiar with the different internal blockers, you can do some further self-reflection by completing the Survey of The High Performance Mindset: Blockers.

SURVEY OF THE HIGH PERFORMANCE MINDSET: BLOCKERS

Instructions: Please indicate how often you experience the following emotions and behaviours at work, home and in other places.

		Never	Rarely	Some times	Not Sure	Often	Almost Always	Always	Your Score
Feeling anxious									
1	I worry a lot about what others think of me.	1	2	3	4	5	6	7	
2	I lack confidence in being able to get the really hard things done.	1	2	3	4	5	6	7	
3	I feel nervous and restless when I think about what I should be doing.	1	2	3	4	5	6	7	
4	I worry a lot about making mistakes and not being successful at what I'm doing.	1	2	3	4	5	6	7	
5	I feel insecure in doing my job (work, home).	1	2	3	4	5	6	7	
Feeling down									
1	I think of myself as totally hopeless when I see myself put off things I should be doing.	1	2	3	4	5	6	7	
2	When I compare what others have accomplished with what I haven't, I can think "I'm a real loser".	1	2	3	4	5	6	7	
3	I really give myself a hard time when I waste time on unimportant things.	1	2	3	4	5	6	7	
4	I get down on myself for not being as successful as I think I should be.	1	2	3	4	5	6	7	
5	I can get down when people are critical of how I do things.	1	2	3	4	5	6	7	
Feeling angry									
1	I get extremely angry when I am given something unfair to do.	1	2	3	4	5	6	7	
2	I find myself getting back at people who are unsupportive or critical of me.	1	2	3	4	5	6	7	
3	I feel like lashing out when I am not given recognition for doing good work.	1	2	3	4	5	6	7	
4	I can go on a work slowdown when I find people looking after their own interests and forgetting about mine or the project at hand.	1	2	3	4	5	6	7	
5	I feel really angry when I've done a good job and only receive critical comments.	1	2	3	4	5	6	7	

Procrastination									
1	I put off until tomorrow what I should be doing today.	1	2	3	4	5	6	7	
2	I make excuses for putting off doing things.	1	2	3	4	5	6	7	
3	I think that my life really should be easier, and I shouldn't have to work so hard.	1	2	3	4	5	6	7	
4	I seem to leave things until the last minute.	1	2	3	4	5	6	7	
5	I can't be bothered doing boring and tedious work.	1	2	3	4	5	6	7	

Blocker Summary: Which performance blockers interfere with your ability to handle tough situations (e.g., dealing with a difficult person, coping with a challenging task, unrealistic deadlines, change, not getting enough support, criticism)?

____ anxiety ____ feeling down ____ anger ____procrastination

STEPS FOR OVERCOMING BLOCKERS

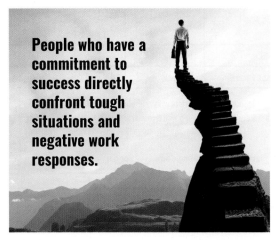

People who have a commitment to success directly confront tough situations and negative work responses.

People who demonstrate a high performance mindset are aware of how they respond in a tough situation, especially of negative emotions and behaviours that block them from resolving the situation – they are aware of how they think, feel and act.

When they observe blockers that get in the way of their ability to deal with a situation or solve a problem, they move decisively to eliminate their own blocker(s) as quickly as possible. Once reduced or eliminated, they are able to sort out the best way to handle the tough situation in a positive and productive fashion.

The following steps can be taking to overcome an internal blocker.

Step 1.	Select a tough situation at home, work or elsewhere where you do not operate at your best.
Step 2.	Identify a blocker (anger, worry, feeling down, procrastination) that is interfering with your ability to resolve or put up with the tough situation.
Step 3.	Decide to directly confront the tough situation and to overcome the blocker.
Step 4.	Develop a plan for overcoming the blocker.
Step 5.	Give the plan a week. If you are not successful, keep employing different strategies and ideas for overcoming the blocker.

To give you a running start, you can review the various tips provided in the following pages for overcoming each of the four blockers.

TIPS FOR OVERCOMING BLOCKERS

ANXIETY

When faced with a difficult person, or challenging person, and you notice yourself getting uptight (sweating, rapid heartbeat, shaking voice):

1. Prepare yourself ahead of time with what to think and what to do using the following self-talk.
"Just think about what I have to do. That's better than worrying."
"No negative self-talk, think positively!"
"Use a few calming, slow breaths to settle nerves."
"It's important to maintain my focus."
"I'll just psyche myself up – I can meet this challenge."
"One step at a time, I can handle this situation."
"I'm starting to get uptight; just relax. Focus on what I want to say."
"Even though the situation is tough, it's not the worst thing that could happen."
"I can cope with this situation."

2. Use physical relaxation skills such as slow deep breathing or tensing – relaxing muscle groups to stay calm.

3. Self-talk to help you reduce worry (select ones that apply to you).
"While it is very desirable to achieve well and to be recognised by others, I do not need achievement or recognition to survive and be happy."
"Mistakes and rejections are inevitable. I will work hard at accepting myself while disliking my mistakes or setbacks."
"My performance at work – perfect or otherwise – does not determine my worth as a person."
"Things are rarely as bad, awful or catastrophic as I imagine them to be."

FEELING DOWN

When you have made a mistake, not achieved your goal, said something stupid, not been acknowledged for a job well done, received criticism or negative feedback:

1. Put an end to self-deprecation. Suppose I said to a Martian, "I'm talking to this intelligent Earthling and he's devoutly believing 'One of my behaviours stinks so therefore, I am a stinker.' Let's suppose the Martian is intelligent, perceptive and rational. What would he think about this Earthling?

Probably, "How can he be so nutty? His behaviour stinks, but he has millions of behaviours and they are all different and all tend to change. How can he, therefore, rate his self, his totality?" The Martian would be right. (quote from Albert Ellis)

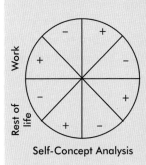

Self-Concept Analysis

2. Complete a self-concept analysis of yourself by writing in your positive characteristics at work and the rest of your life in the (+)s and your negative characteristics at work and the rest of your life in the (-)s. You will see that like all humans, you have many fine qualities and areas for improvement. Do you lose your positive qualities when something bad happens? Does it make sense to rate your overall self-worth based on just one or more negative characteristics?

3. Self-talk to stop feeling down (select ones that can help you).
"I accept who I am, even though I may not like some of my traits and behaviours."
"There are many things about me that I like and do well."
"I have done many things at work successfully in the past, I will succeed in the future."
"I am intelligent and talented enough to learn what I have to do and how to do it in order to accomplish my goals."
"My performance at work – perfect or otherwise – does not determine my worth as a person."
"I am confident that everything will turn out okay given that I have my goals, know what to do, and work hard."
"I prefer people to like me, but I can live without their approval."
"Mistakes and setbacks are inevitable. I will accept myself while disliking my mistakes and setbacks."

ANGER

When confronted with unfairness, inconsideration, disrespect and someone letting you down:
1. Focus your thinking away from the person and what he/she has done/not done. Remind yourself about the negative consequences for you when you get very angry.

2. Be aware when you gradually start to become angry and tense.

3. Use self-talk that can help you to feel less angry (select ones that apply to you).
"While it is preferable to be treated fairly, kindly and considerately, there is no law of the universe that says I must be."
"Anger does not help me in the long run."
"I can cope successfully with unfair people though I would prefer they behave better."
"People are the way they are because that's the way they are. Tough."
"People are fallible and will often, but not always, do the wrong thing. That's the way fallible human beings work."

4. Employ a relaxation skill (deep breathing, positive mental visualisation, yoga) to manage your physical tenseness.

5. To request a change in behaviour from someone. You should:
(a) describe the behaviour you see and/or hear in the other person using descriptive rather than attacking words,
(b) (optional) express the feelings you experience as a result of the other person's behaviour,
(c) ask for specific changes in behaviour, and
(d) spell out the positive consequences for the person of his/her changing behaviour and the negative consequences if he/she does not.

6. When you keep control of your anger, pay close attention to the positive consequences for you.

PROCRASTINATION

When you are faced with work tasks that need to be done and which you consider to be boring, time – consuming and frustrating:

1. Excuses: (select those that apply to you and stamp them out)

"I don't have time to do this today. It will be easier for me to do it tomorrow."

"I'll do it as soon as other things in my life have cleared up."

"Since I do my best work under pressure, I'll just postpone this until the pressure builds."

"Once I did something just before deadline and it worked out well; I'll do it at the last minute again."

"There's no point in starting if I don't know how to do this job properly."

"How can I be expected to finish a project that I've lost interest in?"

2. Techniques
- The knockout technique. The harder and more distasteful a task, the better it is to do it immediately.
- Worst-first approach. Identify the most difficult part of the task and do it first.
- Bits and pieces approach. Do anything you want in connection with the task you want to accomplish. Gradually do more and more until the task itself doesn't seem so impossible.
- Five minute plan. Take a task you've been procrastinating over and work on it a minimum of five minutes. Once you've finished five minutes then you can set yourself another five minutes and then another.
- Establish a set time. Schedule a fixed time to begin the work tasks you have been putting off doing.

3. Self-talk for overcoming procrastination: "In order to achieve pleasant results in the long-term, I sometimes have to do unpleasant things in the short-term. I can stand things I don't like to do. Compared to the worst things that could happen, how bad is it having to do this work?"

THE PERFORMANCE CYCLE

THE WORK PERFORMANCE CYCLE

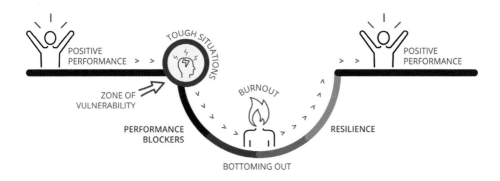

Have a look at how people perform their tasks at work or home – what I call "The Performance Cycle". To begin with, we strive as much as possible to do the best we can. We aspire to perform at high levels in order to achieve our goals including bringing up our kids, relating to our partner and doing our best on the job.

However, on any day – at work and home – we are confronted with different tough situations that threaten our capacity to manage and solve problems effectively.

Those situations that temporarily exceed our capacity to cope and which can create loads of stress enter what I call our "zone of vulnerability".

At work, common tough situations that can enter our zone of vulnerability include time-work overload including too much to do and not enough time to do it; colleagues who behave inconsiderately or unprofessionally; challenging work demands; unfair organisational practices; change and receiving criticism or a negative work evaluation.

At home, events that can populate your zone of vulnerability include financial pressures, not receiving enough support, overload, criticism and disagreements with your partner and difficult problems your kids experience.

At these times, you can experience a number of different "blockers" that can, until sorted, drive us into a downward spiral. As reviewed, these include excess anger, anxiety, feeling very down and procrastination. If the problems continue and you have long-standing levels of stress you can burn out.

Over time, as can be seen in the upward trend in the green arrows, we regain emotional calmness and control until we get back on top. It can also be seen in The Performance Cycle illustration that in some instances, the failure to become aware of our negative work responses, combined with ongoing and unresolved tough situations, can result in burnout.

The Enhanced Performance Cycle

THE ENHANCED WORK PERFORMANCE CYCLE

The performance cycle of people with a high performance mindset has a different look. The high performance mindset produces very high levels of positivity and productivity in order to deal with the many challenges and people they work with.

Here's the important point. Due to their very strong Commitment to Success, Others and Self, people with a high performance mindset perceive far fewer situations as overwhelming their ability to cope and manage. Strong commitments to success, others and self lead to strong self-efficacy and self-belief. As a result, they perform at consistently high levels.

And when people encounter tough situations that fall in their zone of vulnerability, they respond less negatively. Because of their mindset, they are less prone to experience a significant downward slide in their performance.

Why? As you can see from the "enhanced performance cycle", when they become aware of blockers, they engage their resilience to remain calm, in control and as a result, they stop the downward flow of their performance. They spend less time getting angry, down or worrying and they definitely avoid procrastination. They maintain a focus on seeking solutions to tough situations.

Finally, and this is what distinguishes the results of highly successful and fulfilled mums, dads, kids, colleagues, managers, etc., they continuously learn something from their experience so that the next time a similar tough situation arises, they go one better.

The great news is that everyone can develop their mindset and it makes a big difference.

CASE STUDY:
JORDIE BLAKE GOES ONE BETTER

It is two months later and Jordie is sitting in a chair to the left side of centre stage. He surveys the audience, some 300 advertising account managers representing their companies at the event that he has helped put together. He replays in his mind: "Well, she was right, I do have what it takes to be successful …We'll pick up at least three new accounts from this and I have to admit, it does feel good. The more I focus on what I can do, the better I become."

On cue, he stands up to wind up the promotional event and invite his guests to stay for drinks, nibbles and networking. As he leaves the stage and heads for the function room his mind drifts back to the last meeting with Agatha, his boss. He remembers how he felt going into that meeting and for that matter, coming out. Her terse message had been "get your finger out Jordie – get to work on what we pay you to do or go – just don't waste our time." He had been given a choice – walk away or face the demon and slay it. Jordie had left the meeting gritting his teeth and making a decision: "I can do this, I will do this, I am successful…"

Jordie takes a detour to the gents to freshen up and looks at himself in the mirror: "It wasn't her, it was me. I was paying out on everyone because I didn't want to put myself on the line with stuff I don't like doing… It's true what they say, short term pain for long term gain. Persistence has worked – bagging myself over my lack of performance and taking her criticism as failure only made the whole situation ten times worse. It's like the more I started to need her approval, the more stressed I became. I had to chill out and stop taking everything she said so personally… I didn't think I could do it, but I could, and what's more I am still doing it and doing it well…" He takes a deep breath, adjusts his tie and heads out to join the group.

Jordie visualised his desk from six weeks ago. Scattered files, messy desktop, and paperwork and clutter everywhere. He had been drowning in a cacophony of "work in progress" all of which needed immediate attention. After his second meeting with Agatha, he had grimly buckled down to clear his workspace and systematically deal with issues he had been avoiding for weeks. Slowly method crept back in and the funny thing was that once he had started to get organised and to really focus on the work, it had gotten better and better. Actively managing his time and schedule had bought Jordie increased capacity and his productivity had soared.

From the corner of his eye Jordie spots Bill Williams, the senior business journalist from the BRW. He has an idea and approaches him. "Hey Bill, great to see you – I've got someone I would like you to meet." He grabs Bill by the elbow and steers him towards Agatha. "Bill this is Agatha, my manager – she is the mastermind behind Pure Concept's new direction. You might like to have a chat and see what she has to say – Agatha, this is Bill, he writes for the BRW." Agatha turns and smiles at Jordie and Bill and immediately seizes the opportunity Jordie has thrown her way.

Jordie heads to the bar feeling more than moderately pleased with himself. "She's tough, she's often unfair but I don't have to let her push my emotional buttons, I am the one who is in charge of how I feel and what I do, no one else! My lack of performance was making her look bad and I just didn't care. But this will make her look good. No way am I going down that path again, I might not like her behaviour but for me to get where I want to go, I have to accept her warts and all rather than dismiss her as a total drop kick – after all, she has put points on the board."

It had taken him a month to come up with the strategy and he remembers the pitch we discussed: "Look Agatha, I may not like doing this stuff but nothing ventured, nothing gained. If it bombs, at least I had a go. Anyway, I reckon it will succeed and if it doesn't, at least we will learn from the experience and then we will get the next one right." To his surprise, Agatha had backed the idea and sold it to senior management. "We'll run with it Jordie but this had better be the start of more like it. I don't want to lose your creative skills but they must be combined with the business development stuff. OK?"

He picks up his champagne and sips it slowly, savouring the moment. Ben Henderson from Comet Pty Ltd approaches him and says, "Hey Jordie, great gig – I reckon you'll get some results from this – good one mate." Jordie grins, "There are two things you can count on mate, we are all going to die and things will always keep changing – I just want to drive the change where I can and stop freaking out when I can't."

Jordie turns, grabs a plate and starts to circulate, offering guests some blotter for the champagne. He bumps into Kerry McGuire who works in Public Relations at Pure Concept. "Hey Jordie, better give me one of those while we can still afford them." This is delivered with more than a bit of edge and Jordie, who knows Kerry well, pulls her aside. "What's up? You seem a little stressed." "I do? How surprising given the fallout from Attila the Hun over there (she gestures to Agatha who is still talking to Bill Williams). Do you realise what this new direction is costing us? Revenue is down and Shrivers has withdrawn completely. I mean Shrivers was one of yours wasn't it? And Dot Point is wobbly too – suddenly questioning our capacity to deliver – how can we get new customers and still provide the same level of service to our core clients? She just doesn't get it – it's all about relationships, we need to keep everyone happy as well as pulling new business. How can you look so calm and confident when we are on the brink of disaster because some jumped up yuppie decided we need to change strategies to make her look good. She has no idea how much strain this is placing on my section."

Jordie gives a wry smile, "Well I wasn't exactly calm a few weeks ago but I have learned a couple of things in recent times. Maybe I can help. First, change and unpredictability are a fact of life. Instead of freaking out, refusing to budge and giving myself an ulcer, I made a decision – I was going to succeed no matter what, so I calmed myself down and then put my energy into getting the best possible result that I could rather than spinning my wheels about decisions that had already been made... it wasn't until I put things into perspective that I stopped panicking."

Kerry nods, "I guess that I don't feel particularly valued or that she is aware of the degree of difficulty she is creating with her empire building."

"Sounds familiar, I figured out how to get along with her. I can choose how I respond to Agatha, and for that matter, anyone else."

"Yeah I guess so – thanks Jordie – catch you soon."

Jordie turns and drains his glass thinking "I can cope with anything now, the more new clients, the more creative stuff I get to do for them. UK you are a long, long way away."

Lost in thought, Jordie is startled back into the moment by a hand on his arm. "Well done Jordie, we're in next week's edition and by the way, call me Taggie. Can you please schedule a meeting for tomorrow morning first thing please?"

Jordie drops in at the office on the way home and quickly shoots off an email. "Hi Taggie, just wanted to thank you for your support today, Jordie".

The following morning Jordie arrives bright and early to meet with his manager. She has a smile on her face and opens the meeting with "Well I guess you have demonstrated what you actually can do Jordie – congratulations, I wasn't sure you had it in you but now I know you do. Your confidence is now showing. Keep it up and please don't drop the ball again – we certainly don't want to lose you." Jordie smiles and mentally starts to plan his next team briefing.

In Part 4, I discuss resilience, what it is and how to strengthen it in order to further develop your mindset, so you are less stressed, more effective and constantly go one better.

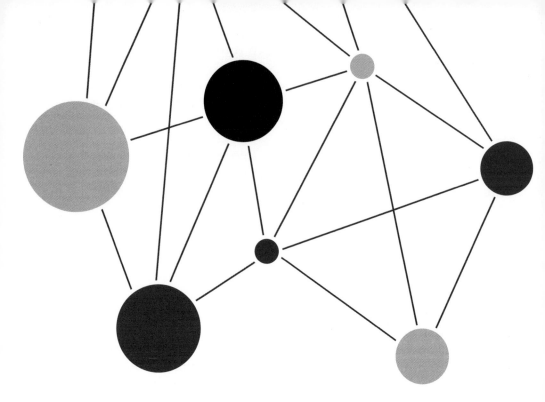

Part 4

Resilience

RESILIENCE

STRENGTH CONFIDENCE MOTIVATE PROTECTING SELF EFFORT CHANGE AGILITY

"Do not judge me by my success, judge me by how
many times I fell down and got back up again."
- Nelson Mandela, apartheid revolutionary,
former president South Africa

"A good half of the art of living is resilience."
- Alain de Botton, British-Swiss philosopher

"When we learn how to become resilient, we learn how to embrace
the beautifully broad spectrum of the human experience."
- Jaeda Dewalt, author, *Chasing Desdemona*

"Successful people demonstrate their resilience
through their dedication to making progress every day,
even if that progress is marginal."
- Jonathan Mills, author, *How to Be Successful in Business and in Life*

"That which does not kill us makes us stronger."
- Friedrich Nietzsche, German philosopher

"No one escapes pain, fear, and suffering. Yet from pain can come
wisdom, from fear can come courage, from suffering can come
strength – if we have the virtue of resilience."
- Eric Greitens, author, *Resilience*

STRESS

PSYCHOLOGICAL SYMPTOMS OF STRESS

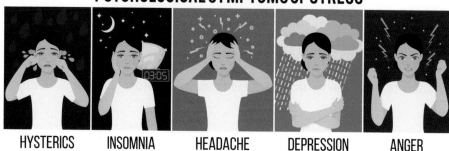

HYSTERICS   INSOMNIA   HEADACHE   DEPRESSION   ANGER

No matter how much talent, skill and determination you have, on any given day, stuff happens that can knock you off the road.

Often, a stressful event can trigger internal blockages and a downward spiral can ensue.

More so than ever, our lives are very stressful. All over the world in our homes and in all occupations stress is on the up.

According to the Mental Health Foundation of the United Kingdom. 74% of adults have felt so stressed at some point over the last year they felt overwhelmed or unable to cope. In Australia, 41% of teachers report high levels of occupational stress.

According to a recent survey of parenting in America, 24 per cent of parents said they had an extreme level of stress over the past month. Young people are quite stressed. My research with the Australian Council for Educational Research has revealed with a sample of over 135,000 students that anxiety has risen from 44% fifteen years ago to 58% today, while levels of stress have risen from 29% to 49%.

And now, the Coronavirus (COVID-19) has also magnified stress for everyone. Fears about COVID-19 can take an emotional toll, especially if you're already living with an anxiety disorder. But you're not powerless. How stressed are you at this very moment? You can judge your level of stress from your emotional, cognitive and physical state.

SIGNS AND SYMPTOMS OF STRESS

Instructions: Tick any signs of stress you have experienced over the past month.

- [ ] Feeling irritable or depressed
- [ ] Disappointment with yourself even when you haven't made mistakes
- [ ] Increased emotional reactions
- [ ] Loss of interest in work
- [ ] Loss of confidence in your abilities
- [ ] Changes in eating habits
- [ ] Problems sleeping
- [ ] Trouble concentrating

- [ ] Muscle tension or headaches
- [ ] Stomach problems
- [ ] Social withdrawal
- [ ] Changes in work attendance
- [ ] Loss of libido
- [ ] Using alcohol or drugs to cope
- [ ] Poor memory
- [ ] Fatigue

Everyone has different stressful, tough situations they encounter at work, home and life that they are vulnerable to which result in negative reactions and a downward spiral in performance.

Maybe your partner continues to say annoying things, your manager continues to overload you with work she could be doing or your kids are constantly fighting.

In today's crazy world of COVID-19, you may be or have been exposed to a large number of tough situations from not being able to spend time with friends at bars and restaurants, having family in self-isolation, or seeing the fear on the faces of your children about what's going on.

Everyone reacts differently to stressful situations. How you respond to the outbreak of the disease and other stressful, tough situations in your life depends on your background, the community you live in and things that make you different from other people.

Wouldn't it be great if an umbrella of sorts could protect you in today's times so you don't feel like you've been soaked in negative feelings or feel stressed out and miserable. It would be so much easier if feeling bad about things could kind of just wash over you.

Well, it's not an umbrella that is going to protect you. But, the good news is that there is something very powerful that DOES protect you from feeling very upset when bad stuff happens.

IT'S YOUR RESILIENCE

RESILIENCE is not something you can buy, borrow – or even steal. It's not something you are born with. But as you develop, you learn a little bit or a great deal about how to be resilient.

So how does one actually become more resilient? How does resilience become wired into your high performance mindset?

You may have picked up clues from your parents, siblings, teachers and friends in terms of how they go about responding to difficulty and pressure.

It's important to have someone to talk to when the going gets tough – someone who's a good listener, who cares but is also good at helping you solve problems.

We also know that the voice inside our head, our self-talk, is really important. When faced with different tough situations, resilient people tell themselves with a strong voice, things like:

"I CAN do this."
"I haven't learned this YET."
"This is NOT the worst thing that could happen."
"I CAN stand what is happening even though I don't like it."
"I am me and that's OK. I ACCEPT who I am."

Resilient people also use a large number of coping skills to help them manage their emotions and behaviour. They know how to:

1. Relax under pressure.
2. Manage their time – they use a diary and they prioritise important things that have to be done soon from those things that can wait until later.
3. Solve conflicts without fighting, by coming up with a good plan of steps to take.
4. Communicate what they are thinking, feeling and wanting, rather than keeping things bottled up inside.
5. Exercise regularly which we know helps us deal with all sorts of mental pressures.

The Resilience Lifesaver (youcandoiteducation.com.au)

- **YOU** — Prepare
- **CAN** — Coping Skills
- **DO** — Action
- **IT!**
- Self-Talk

Prepare: What is the tough situation or problem I am faced with? How do I feel and respond when most stressed? Goals for how I would like to feel and behave the next time it happens.

Self-Talk: "I accept myself no matter what!" "This is not the worst thing that can happen!" "Even though this is bad, I can stand it!" "People who do the wrong things are not totally bad." "I haven't solved this problem YET."

RESILIENCE

Coping Skills: Be aware of how I feel. Be mindful, focus, relax. Exercise, eat sensibly. Find something fun to do. Talk with someone you trust.

Action: Be confident. Persevere. Get myself organised (manage time; set priorities). Strengthen my relationships (be friendly and engage). Problem solve.

My own resilience which continues to develop has been a lifesaver for me in so many ways. At work, it has helped me to respond less negatively when I've had setbacks – for sure! It has helped me stay positive and motivated when faced with criticism. At home, as a parent of two grown-up kids and partner for many years to Patricia, I continuously call on my resilience to deal with everyday problems. And to deal with health issues (and serious injury), again, my resilience has helped me to bounce back.

I have spent over two decades learning from others and my profession ways to manage stress – coping skills and self-talk to help me stay calm, calm down and bounce back.

Many of these resilience "tools" like the Resilience Lifesaver continue to work for me – and I call on when needed. I also have spent years helping others develop their resilience.

CASE STUDY: HELEN TEACHER-LIBRARIAN

I'd like to talk to you about Helen – an amazing person as well as an accomplished teacher-librarian. Helen is married, has two great children and has a variety of outside interests including singing and painting. Recently, for the first time in her work life she experienced intense work stress that was so great she wondered whether she could continue working. The work stressor for Helen was a Year 9 student George, a large, loud, intimidating boy who constantly behaved poorly and disrupted her library class. Helen sought the help of a professional coach, me, to help her manage her stress and deal with George.

Within 90 days, Helen made huge progress where her stress level diminished greatly and George's behaviour improved. Thoughts of early retirement evaporated – even with George still in her class.

She achieved this outcome through strengthening her resilience using a number of stress management tools.

- Re-calibrated the "badness" of stressful events
- Decided not to take what was happening personally
- Relaxed when she noticed she was tensing
- Awoke earlier to exercise; ate breakfast
- Sought support

Here's the resilience tool that seems to be the most popular amongst those who I have coached and presented professional workshops to that helped Helen a lot. I use it often, too – so does my family.

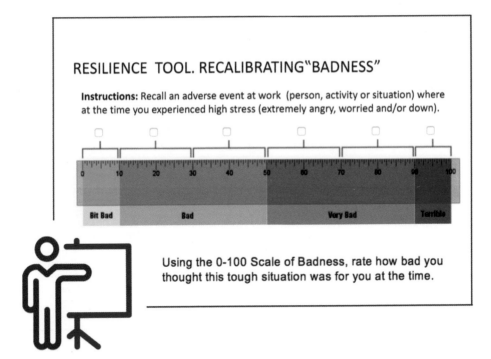

RESILIENCE TOOL. RECALIBRATING"BADNESS"

Instructions: Recall an adverse event at work (person, activity or situation) where at the time you experienced high stress (extremely angry, worried and/or down).

Bit Bad | Bad | Very Bad | Terrible

Using the 0-100 Scale of Badness, rate how bad you thought this tough situation was for you at the time.

Recall a tough situation that occurred at work or home where at the time you found yourself being highly emotionally stressed (please do not select an event that was very traumatic like a suicide). It might have been severe, sharp criticism, an instance of very poor misbehaviour of one of your children, the absence of timely communication from a manager you work for or someone who promises to do something important you need done and doesn't follow through.

Here's a question: At the time you were extremely upset – not now when you may be calmer – how bad was it for you that the tough situation or event had occurred or was occurring? You can use the above 0–100 point Scale of Badness. A rating of 90–100 represents that you were thinking that the event was "Awful and terrible", 50–90 you were thinking "This is very bad", 10–50 represents you thinking that the event was "Bad" and 0–10 means you were thinking that the adversity was "A bit bad". At the time you were extremely upset, what was your rating of how bad the tough situation was on the Scale of Badness?

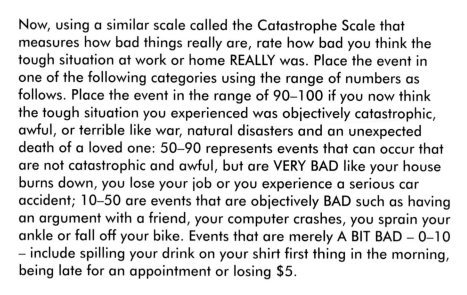

The Catastrophe Scale

Measures how bad things <u>really are</u>. Compared with events on the Catastrophe Scale that are rated as very bad or terrible, what rating of badness would you now give the tough situation at work?

Bit Bad	Bad	Very Bad	Terrible
• Unwashed coffee cup • Pimple • Late for appointment	• Ticket • Cold • Critical comment • Lose wallet	• House fire • Serious illness • Car crash • Loss of job	• War • Natural disaster • Death loved one

Now, using a similar scale called the Catastrophe Scale that measures how bad things really are, rate how bad you think the tough situation at work or home REALLY was. Place the event in one of the following categories using the range of numbers as follows. Place the event in the range of 90–100 if you now think the tough situation you experienced was objectively catastrophic, awful, or terrible like war, natural disasters and an unexpected death of a loved one: 50–90 represents events that can occur that are not catastrophic and awful, but are VERY BAD like your house burns down, you lose your job or you experience a serious car accident; 10–50 are events that are objectively BAD such as having an argument with a friend, your computer crashes, you sprain your ankle or fall off your bike. Events that are merely A BIT BAD – 0–10 – include spilling your drink on your shirt first thing in the morning, being late for an appointment or losing $5.

Compared with events on the Catastrophe Scale that are rated as awful and terrible, 90–100, what rating of badness would you now give the tough situation?

Many people notice that at the time they were very upset about an event at work or home, they rated the event towards the top end of the Catastrophe Scale thinking: "This event is awful, terrible", but using the Catastrophe Scale, they recalibrate how bad the event really was. There is a natural, human tendency to blow the badness of significant events out of proportion.

Catastrophe Scale
measures how bad things really are

youcandoiteducation.com.au
© The Bernard Group

YouCanDoIt!

Helen was catastrophising about George's bad behaviour and her inability to handle him in her class. As she employed the Catastrophe Scale, instead of blowing the badness of the situation out of proportion, she said to me: "Yes, I can see it's bad, but not nearly as bad compared with something seriously happening to a member of my family."

Learning how to keep the badness of adverse events in perspective – thinking "This event is bad but it definitely is not the worst things that can happen" is an important coping skill that when used strengthens resilience and helps you to keep stress at a manageable level.

Now I've learnt that it doesn't matter who you are – whether you are a stay-at-home parent and/or are employed outside of home, whether or not you are a single parent, whether you have one or 12 kids, whether you are getting started in the workforce or have been going for 20 years – and what job sector and your level of responsibility, EVERYONE can benefit from strengthening their resilience.

I hope you will share with others what you are learning in this book about Resilience. Why not start with sharing the Catastrophe Scale?

RESILIENCE. THE BIG PICTURE

Here's a definition I use for resilience.

When faced with challenging, demanding or threatening situations including change and when confronted with difficult people:

1. Being aware of your emotions (anxiety, anger, down) including your degree of upset.
2. Being able to prevent yourself from getting extremely upset.
3. When you get extremely upset, being able to control your behaviour so that you do not behave aggressively or withdraw from others for too long a time.
4. When you are very upset, knowing what to do to calm down within a reasonable period of time.
5. Bouncing back to the tough situation to solve the problem and go one better.

The important elements of resilience are 1. of your emotions and behaviour when highly upset and 2. bouncing back to the stressful, tough situation within a reasonable period of time.

Resilience is not about eliminating emotions totally. It is about empowering you so that you feel you have some control over your emotional response in tough situations.

The accompanying survey will enable you to determine the strength of your resilience.

SELF-SURVEY: RESILIENCE

Instructions: Please indicate how often in tough, demanding and challenging situations and when working with difficult people you behave in the following ways at work.

		Almost Never	Sometimes	Often	Almost Always	YOUR SCORE
1	I am aware of my feelings when I am confronted with a tough situation (significant criticism, my sub-standard performance, incompetent or unfair behaviour of others).	1	2	3	4	
2	I can be very intolerant and judgmental of someone who does the wrong thing including not doing things the way they should be done.	4	3	2	1	
3	I stay calm when I am faced with extremely challenging work with tough deadlines, when interacting with difficult people, or having to make sudden, unexpected adjustments to meet changing priorities.	1	2	3	4	
4	I tend to blow things out of proportion.	4	3	2	1	
5	When I notice that my emotional level is too high, I am able to make adjustments so that I become calmer and in control.	1	2	3	4	
6	I find myself thinking, "I can't stand this situation or person's behaviour."	4	3	2	1	
7	When I am in the middle of a tough situation and I find myself very angry, anxious or down, I am very good at controlling my behaviour. I don't escalate the situation or withdraw.	1	2	3	4	
8	I am someone who takes things very personally.	4	3	2	1	
9	When I get extremely uptight, stressed, I bounce back quickly.	1	2	3	4	
10	I use one or more coping skills to stay calm (breathing - muscle relaxation, assertion, sense of humour, distraction, mindfulness, gratitude, find someone to talk to).	1	2	3	4	
					TOTAL RESILIENCE SCORE	

The strength of your Resilience is:

under-developed	moderate	developed	well-developed	gold standard
10 - 17	18 - 23	24 - 31	32 - 35	36 - 40

Here's a few ideas about that way we operate mentally that will help illuminate what resilience is and ways to strengthen it.

Insight 1.
Emotions are not like an on-off switch

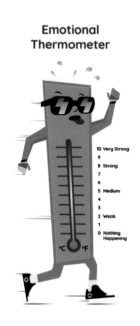

Emotional Thermometer

Emotions do not operate as an on-off switch – either you are anxious or not, angry or not, feel down or not. Here's what we know. When faced with a stressful event, people have choices in the degree of emotional upset they experience.

The Emotional Thermometer shows that you can have different degrees of a feeling from almost nothing when something bad (or good) happens to being extremely upset where you register a temperature at the top of the thermometer.

Generally, no matter the seriousness of the tough situation or event, when we get extremely – or some might say overly upset – not only can we be in a whole lot of emotional pain when we feel highly anxious or down, but our ability to think clearly and respond effectively is greatly diminished. And feeling nothing when faced with a tough situation is not so good as we lose the emotional energy needed to do something about the situation – if we can!

So, for me, when I'm faced with a stressor, I monitor my emotions and try to avoid getting to the top of the Emotional Thermometer. And when I do get to the top of my Emotional Thermometer I try to calm down as quickly as possible.

An example is when someone promises they will get back to me on something we agreed is important and they would do so within 24 hours and I do not hear back from them. As time ticks by, I notice my emotional temperature rising from irritation and annoyance to feeling more angry. I use this awareness to keep myself from getting really angry as I know this will lead to negative consequences in the long-term.

Insight 2.
External events trigger stress

Stress comes from specific tough situations and scenarios. What's interesting is that these differ from person to person. Some of the scenarios common across people have to do with when your job expectations and responsibilities exceed your existing skillset – plus you are not given enough support. Other tough situations – like someone being rude – might not strongly effect you as much as it would another.

Resilience building starts with you identifying your external sources of stress and then preparing to confront them by identifying strategies to manage them.

One way to do this is to make a list of the tough situations in your zone of vulnerability that trigger your negative and unhelpful reactions.

To pinpoint those events in your Zone of Vulnerability, you can complete the *Inventory of Tough Situations at Work and the Inventory of Tough Situations at Home*.

INVENTORY OF TOUGH SITUATIONS AT WORK

Instructions: This survey will help you to become aware of tough situations you experience that can have a negative impact on your stress and performance. Tough situations refer to tasks, events and people that temporarily challenge or exceed people's capacity to cope. Typically, they respond to these situations with anger, anxiety, feeling down and/or procrastination. Tick YES or NO to indicate which of the situations you experience as tough. Also, in the blank space provided at the end of each section, please add specific examples of tough situations that are not listed. You can leave blank those questions that do not apply.

I	Challenging Work Demands	YES	NO
1	Excessive hours of work.		
2	Unrealistic deadlines.		
3	Unrealistic work expectations imposed by others.		
4	Work encroaches on your personal/family time.		
5	Too much work to do, not enough time to do it.		
6	Having to write reports.		
7	New technologies you are expected to master.		
8	Public speaking.		
9	Providing performance appraisal/review to others.		
OTHER			

II	Relationship Difficulties	YES	NO
1	Personality clash with a team member.		
2	Being ignored by a colleague.		
3	Team member who does not pull weight and/or does not follow through on what he/she says.		
4	Verbal harassment by someone you work with.		
5	Not being supported by people you work with.		
6	Client who is negative towards you and who may undermine your best efforts.		
7	Team member who does not volunteer to lend a hand.		
8	Colleague who appears to be undermining your success.		
9	Gossip and rumours being spread about you.		
10	Exclusion from social group after work.		
OTHER			

III	"Unfair" Organisational Practices	YES	NO
1	Poor communication from senior management.		
2	Not being consulted over a decision which effects your work.		
3	Lack of independence/autonomy.		
4	Confusion over role and responsibilities.		

INVENTORY OF TOUGH SITUATIONS AT WORK

III	"Unfair" Organisational Practices (Cont.)	YES	NO
5	Negative ways in which performance reviews are conducted.		
6	Not being provided with necessary supplies/equipment.		
7	Few opportunities for promotion.		
8	Not enough professional development for what you do.		
OTHER			

IV	Change	YES	NO
1	Change in who you work with (team members).		
2	Change in management.		
3	Change in your work responsibilities and expectations.		
4	Change in additional number of things you are expected to handle.		
5	Change in way in which your performance is evaluated.		
OTHER			

V	Work Performance Issues	YES	NO
1	Not achieving one or more goals you have set.		
2	Being criticised.		
3	Receiving a relatively poor performance review.		
4	Making mistakes.		
5	Being passed over for promotion.		
OTHER			

Note the three or four situations listed that are in your Zone of Vulnerability (those events that occasion highest levels of stress).

INVENTORY OF TOUGH SITUATIONS AT HOME

Instructions: This survey will help you to become aware of tough situations you experience at home that can have a negative impact on your stress and performance, Tough situations refer to tasks, events and people that temporarily challenge or exceed people's capacity to cope. Typically, they respond to these situations with anger, anxiety, feeling down and/or procrastination. Circle YES or NO to indicate which of the situations you experience as tough. Also, in the blank space provided at the end of each section, please add specific examples of tough situations that are not listed. You can leave blank those questions that do not apply.

I	Time/Workload Pressures	YES	NO
1	Not enough time in the week to prepare meals.		
2	Home and garden maintenance.		
3	Not having enough support.		
4	Being a single parent.		
5	Having a very young child.		
6	Being a part-time carer of a family member.		
7	No time for socialising.		
8	No time for exercising regularly.		
9	Have to cut back on personal hobbies.		
10	Too much clutter (stacks of papers, dishes, toys) around house.		
OTHER			

II	Children	YES	NO
1	Not enough time spent with my child(ren).		
2	One of my children has a behaviour problem.		
3	One of my children has a developmental disability (e.g., autism).		
4	My children continuously fight with each other.		
5	My child is receiving poor grades at school.		
6	My child is being bullied at school.		
7	My child doesn't seem to have any close friends.		
8	One of my children is unwell.		
9	My child's demands are overwhelming.		
OTHER			

III	Partner/Spouse	YES	NO
1	Being too busy to spend time with each other and share responsibilities.		
2	Intimacy and sex rare due to busy, health problems, and any number of other reasons.		
3	You and your partner are not communicating effectively.		
4	You and/or partner are consuming too much alcohol and/or using drugs.		
5	My partner is unwilling to do his/her share of housework.		

INVENTORY OF TOUGH SITUATIONS AT HOME

III	Partner/Spouse (Cont.)	YES	NO
6	My partner has health issues and cannot cope.		
7	My partner spends too much time on personal interests. (e.g., regularly comes home very late from golf, cycling, video games).		
8	Having too many arguments with partner.		
9	Unbalanced sharing of communal items (TV, radio, car, computer).		
OTHER			

IV	Extended Family	YES	NO
1	Little time to stay connected with family.		
2	Unrealistic expectations from extended family members.		
3	Little or no support from family members, (e.g., help with babysitting, serious illness in family).		
4	Little positive acknowledgement from family members, criticised all the time.		
5	Family celebrations ignored by extended family members (e.g., birthdays).		
6	Extended family do not approve or acknowledge my partner or children from another person.		
OTHER			

V	Finances	YES	NO
1	Arguing about money.		
2	Not enough money to meet regular bills.		
3	Setting and keeping to a budget.		
4	Blaming other for monetary losses.		
5	Spending too much money on non-necessities (e.g., gambling, smoking, beauty visits).		
6	Disagreeing on expenditure on household items (e.g., purchase of appliance).		
7	Partner refuses to allow access to money or expects me to account for every cent.		
OTHER			

Note the three or four of the situations listed that are in your Zone of Vulnerability (those events that occasion highest levels of stress).

Insight 3.
"Thinking Makes it So"

This insight is the most important.

Epictetus, a Stoic-Romain philosopher, wrote in the second century, A.D., that "People are not effected by events but by the view they take of events." The above quote by Shakespeare (Hamlet, Act 2, Scene 2) mirrors the same idea; namely, how we interpret and evaluate experiences largely determines how we feel and behave.

The illustration represents this idea in pictorial form. Things that happen to us get funnelled into our brains. Before we respond, we spend a little bit or a lot of time thinking about what is happening. The thinking we have causes us to feel in certain ways which then leads us to behave as we do.

The point here is that while it seems that outside events cause feelings, the events do not directly cause our feelings. So, to say someone or something "makes" you really upset (or not upset) is not the way our emotions operate.

It's possible to view this relationship using an ABC model developed by the world famous psychologist, Albert Ellis.

THE ABCS OF SELF-MANAGEMENT

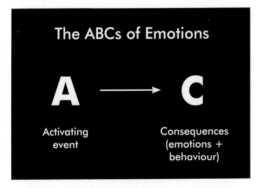

Many people believe that what happens to them – referred to in the diagram as "Activating event" – causes them to feel and behave in the way they do. This can be quite disempowering since it appears that our emotional lives and how we behave are not under our control, but caused by outside events.

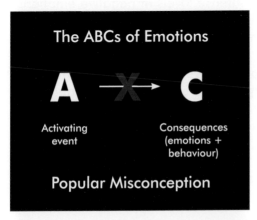

This view is a misconception. Activating events that we experience (the "A" in the diagram) do not cause our emotional and behavioural consequences (the "C" in the diagram).

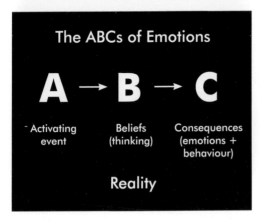

As you see in the diagram, it is the "B", our beliefs, our thinking, our self-talk about "A"that causes "C" our feelings and behaviour.

The work of scientists studying brain function as well as from psychologists working with people with mental health issues has also revealed two types of thinking which operate from two different parts of the brain that influence how we feel and behave in very different ways.

We have also learnt that everyone has a tendency and capacity to think in two different ways about the same thing and that two different people can think and therefore feel quite differently about the same tough situation as a result of the way each thinks.

One way we think is helpful in dealing with tough situations, the other way is not.

One way of thinking creates very intense levels of negative emotions and behaviours, the other way leads to a calmer approach to life's difficulties and greater effectiveness.

Our dysfunctional way to think about adversity Albert Ellis termed "irrational" while the helpful way to think Ellis termed "rational."

Below, you will an example of these two ways of thinking on how we feel.

The scenario illustrated is of an employee who was bullied by his manager.

You can see that when confronted with a tough situation of being unfairly criticised, the employee in the above illustrations can adopt ways of thinking that either lead to heightened emotional and behavioural responses or thinking (left picture) or thinking that leads to self-management and calmness in the face of adversity (right picture).

When you notice that your emotional temperature is getting quite high, you will want to recognise those aspects of your self-talk that are over-charging your emotional battery and change them. At these times, you will want to make sure, as much as possible, that the objective, flexible and sensible side of your thinking is turned up the loudest.

CHALLENGING AND CHANGING THE WAY YOU THINK

When you become aware that your self-talk is quite rigid, extreme and not exactly true, you can make a conscious shift in your thinking so that your self-talk is more flexible, moderate and objective by asking yourself three questions:

Is what I am thinking sensible or logical?
Is what I am thinking true?
Is what I am thinking helping me?

Example 1.
"I can't stand having to do this paperwork."
This thinking is clearly an extreme evaluation that doesn't really hold water. Even though you don't like paperwork, in fact, the evidence is that you have and will continue to survive all things associated with administration and form filing.
Change self-talk: "I don't like paperwork, but I can stand it."

Example 2.
"It would be awful and horrible if I said something stupid or people laughed. I'll just keep quiet."
This thinking is clearly extreme. "Awful" and "horrible" mean the worst things in the world that could happen. Obviously, making what others may think as a silly comment is bad, but objectively not catastrophic, not even very bad compared to really serious life occurrences including serious illness, natural disasters, terrorism and the like.
Change self-talk to: "It's not the end of the world if people laugh at what I say."

Example 3.
"When I have made mistakes or performed imperfectly, that shows I am hopeless, a loser, a failure."

This type of thinking, which is not uncommon, is not sensible. Non-achievement in one or more areas of work never equates to you being a total non-achiever and failure in all areas of your life. It is also not true (no evidence) to justify concluding you are totally hopeless.

Change self-talk: "I am a fallible human being who will inevitably make mistakes. While I strive to do my best, I will not always be successful and when I'm not, I am still proud of who I am."

Example 4.

"He (or she) should act more fairly and considerately towards me. Because he (or she) has not, that shows what a total 'idiot' he (or she) is."

This self-talk is quite extreme because while it is preferable that people are considerate and fair and treat you as nicely as you treat them, occasionally for different reasons they will not. It doesn't make sense to think of them at these times as totally bad people. Don't judge people by their sins. Everyone makes mistakes and has fallibilities; they also have their good sides.

Change self-talk: "I prefer people to act decently, but when they don't, they don't. Tough. I won't condemn them as people, I'll just focus on seeing if I can get them to change their behaviour and if I cannot, I can move on."

The battle between positive and negative attitudes

We are all born with two opposing ways of thinking. The degree to which we become stressed when adverse events happen is governed largely by whether we are viewing and interpreting the event through a rational or irrational lens. The accompanying survey will provide you with an opportunity to determine whether you hold any of the major attitudes that lead to poor resilience. Keep in mind that all of us to greater or lesser extents harbour these attitudes. Fortunately, by becoming aware of those that you hold, you have an opportunity to replace the irrational, negative attitudes with positive, rational ones described in the Check Up from Your Neck Up Survey (next page).

YOUR CHECK UP FROM THE NECK UP SURVEY

Instructions: Select the option that indicates your type of thinking when you are faced with adversity.

	Self-Downing When things go badly and I make mistakes or people are critical of me, I tend to put myself down and think of myself as a failure or a loser.	vs	**Accepting Myself** When things go badly and I make mistakes or people are critical of me, I accept myself and do not put myself down at these times.	
	Need for Approval I seem to be someone who is overly concerned with what others think of me, and I think it is terrible to be criticised or thought badly of.	vs	**Being Independent** While I like to be approved of, I don't need the approval of others.	
	Need for Achievement (Perfectionism) I seem to be someone who needs to be highly successful. It is horrible for me to make mistakes.	vs	**Responsible Risk Taking** While I like to be successful, I don't need to be all the time. I try new things even though there is a high likelihood that I might not be successful the first time.	
	I Can't Do It I am a pessimist believing things will turn out for the worst.	vs	**I Can Do It** I generally believe I will be successful and things will turn out for the best.	
	I Can't Be Bothered I really can't stand it when I have too much work to do and not enough time to do it. Things shouldn't be so hard and unpleasant.	vs	**Working Tough** While I prefer that things go comfortably and easily, I accept that in order to achieve pleasant results in the long term, I sometimes have to do unpleasant things in the short term.	
	Not Accepting Everyone People should always act fairly, considerately, and respectfully. I can't stand it when they do not. People who act unfairly are "louses" who deserve to be punished.	vs	**Accepting Everyone** People are fallible and sometimes make mistakes. While I strongly prefer others to act fairly and considerately, I can stand it when they do not. I try hard not to condemn them for their actions.	

The impact of the different ways of thinking on your emotional responses when faced with adversity is represented below.

The impact of the thinking in the left-hand column on your emotional responses when faced with tough situations is represented below.

1. Self-downing
You are prone to feeling down and inadequate.

2. Need for approval
You are prone to social anxiety.

3. Need for achievement (perfectionism)
You are prone to performance anxiety.

4. I can't do it!
You are prone to getting down and feeling helpless and hopeless.

5. I can't be bothered
You are prone to anger when faced with being required to do unpleasant tasks; you may tend to procrastinate in these areas.

6. Not accepting everyone
You are prone to anger with people you perceive as doing the wrong thing.

So, the three takeaways concerning resilience are:

Insight 1. Emotions are not like an on-off switch.

This means that you have a choice in how upset you get when you are faced with a tough situation including not getting your way. At these times, your goal needs to be managing your emotions (staying in the middle of the Emotional Thermometer range) in order to think clearly so you continue to operate at your best.

Insight 2. External events trigger stress

It is good to be clear on what those events are that trigger your very high levels of stress and result in a downward spiral in behaviour. By identifying which tough situations are in your zone of vulnerability, we can prepare ourselves with resilient ways of thinking and coping skills to use to stay calm, cool and effective.

Insight 3 "Thinking makes it so"

People with a high performance mindset take responsibility for how they feel and behave without blaming others or the outside world. They avoid negativity and extreme forms of thinking and, instead, adopt a more realistic, moderate, flexible way to interpret adversity.

STRENGTHENING RESILIENCE: THREE-STEP ACTION PLAN

The following three-step plan is based on the principle that developing resilience is a process that involves working on your response to specific tough situations one situation at a time. As you deploy your resilience successfully, you can then apply the three steps to different tough situations until resilience becomes your new default response.

Writing down a plan for strengthening your resilience can be very helpful in getting started. You can enter your ideas in an **Individual Action Plan: Strengthening your Resilience**.

STEP 1:
TAKE STOCK

To begin with, focus on identifying events that occur at work and home that can sometimes create lots of stress and have a negative impact on your performance. As I've said, those events occupy what is called your Zone of Vulnerability. You can refer to the inventories of tough situations you may have completed earlier.

Resilient people have taken stock of which events they find very stressful – those events that are in their Zone of Vulnerability..

In your Individual Action Plan (next page), you can complete Step 1. Take Stock. Indicate the blockers you can experience on your worst days. Then, reflect on the changes you'd like to see in how you respond should the tough or similar situation occur in the future.

INDIVIDUAL ACTION PLAN: STRENGTHENING YOUR RESILIENCE

Step 1: Take Stock

Identify a 'significant' tough situation at work where you get extremely stressed and where your performance suffers. You can review the results of your Inventory of Tough Situations (Work, Home).

Tough Situation (describe)_____

Which blocker(s) do you need to eliminate?

□ anger   □ anxiety   □ feeling down   □ procrastination

The next time you are confronted with the same or similar tough situation, how would you like to feel and behave?

□ calm   □ hopeful   □ relaxed
□ assertive   □ confident   □ energetic
□ positive   □ determined

Step 2: Take Control

What examples of self-talk can you use to be self-managing of your emotions and behaviour?

□ "This is bad, but not awful."   □ "I can cope with this situation."
□ "I've done hard things before, I can do this."   □ "No pain, no gain."
□ "I won't judge this person by his/her behaviour." □ "I accept myself no matter what."
□ "I'll do the best I can."

Other examples of self-talk you can use: _____

_____

Which coping skills will you use to self-manage in order to stay calm or calm down?

□ find someone to talk to   □ exercise   □ be grateful
□ relax   □ figure out how to solve the problem
□ find something fun to do   □ be assertive

Other coping skills you will use to self-manage emotions: _____

_____

INDIVIDUAL ACTION PLAN: STRENGTHENING YOUR RESILIENCE (CONT.)

Step 3: Take Action

Which social-emotional skills will you use the next time the tough situation arises to solve the problem and go one better?

☐ confidence   ☐ persistence   ☐ organisation   ☐ getting along

Concretely describe how you will behave the next time you are faced with the tough situation.

_____

_____

_____

_____

STEP 2: TAKE CONTROL

Once you are aware of how a stressful situation is adversely effecting your feelings and behaviours and how you would rather feel and behave, your focus is on being resilient through switching on the power of your self-talk and coping skills to take control of your emotions and behaviour.

Resilient *Self-Talk*	Resilient *Coping Skills*
"This is bad but not awful."	Find the 'right' someone to talk to (not someone who agrees with everything you say)
"I've done hard things before, I can do this."	Deep breathing and muscle relaxation
"No pain, no gain."	Exercise and good diet
"Don't stew."	Figure out how to solve the problem
"I accept myself no matter what."	Be assertive rather than aggressive or passive when someone does the wrong thing
"I won't judge this person by his/her behaviour."	Finds ways to feel positive – meet with a friend, listen to music, get active
"I can stand things I don't like."	Be empathic: Figure out what's on their mind

There are powerful ways to think that can help you cope with all sorts of tough situations that are in your zone of vulnerability.

Switch on the power of self-talk

Ever hear yourself thinking: "This is awful, I can't stand it!" You might apply this thinking about the behaviour of one your children, a colleague, or manager or the way the company or organisation you work for operates. When your brain tells your body something is awful and you cannot stand it, your emotions go galloping to the top of your Emotional Thermometer. To strengthen your resilience in the face of adverse events, you can remind yourself that things are not as bad as you think they are – they could be a lot worse. Review the Catastrophe Scale presented earlier. You can also remind yourself that you have stood and will continue to stand things that are bad – the evidence is that these events won't kill you, you won't faint.

Listen for your "self-downing" thinking. We have now learned that one type of thinking that undermines people's resilience is when they put themselves down and take things very personally. This extreme and not sensible way of thinking is called "Self-Downing". In order to rebound from criticism and setbacks, you will want to avoid self-criticism as much as possible.

A great way to think to combat self-downing is to be proud of who you are and when you stumble or someone is derogatory, accept yourself unconditionally, "I am me and that's OK. I accept myself no matter what."

On the following page, I have provided a list of the positive self-talk people value using because it helps them to take control of their feelings and behaviours.

THE POWER OF SELF-TALK

Overcoming anxiety
While it is very desirable to achieve well and be recognised by others, I do not need achievement or recognition to survive and be happy.

Mistakes and rejections are inevitable. I will work hard at accepting myself while disliking my mistakes or setbacks.

My performance at work – perfect or otherwise – does not determine my worth as a person.

Things are rarely as bad, awful, or catastrophic as I imagine them to be.

What's the worst thing that can happen? It's not the end of the world if I'm not successful or if someone thinks badly of me.

Overcoming feeling down
I accept who I am, even though I may not like some of my traits and behaviours.

There are many things about me that I like and do well.

I have done many things at work successfully in the past, I will succeed in the future.

I am intelligent and talented enough to learn what I have to do and how to do it in order to accomplish my goals.

My performance at work – perfect or otherwise – does not determine my worth as a person.

I am confident that everything will turn out okay given that I have my goals, know what to do, and work hard.

I prefer people to like me, but I can live without their approval.

Mistakes and setbacks are inevitable. I will accept myself while disliking my mistakes and setbacks.

Things are rarely as bad, awful, or catastrophic as I imagine them to be.

Overcoming anger
While it is preferable to be treated fairly, kindly and considerately, there is no law of the universe that says I must be.

People who act unfairly, inconsiderately, or unkindly may deserve to be penalised, but never to be totally condemned as rotten no-goodniks who deserve to be eternally damned.

Anger does not help in the long run; it is only temporarily effective at best.

Anger towards others frequently prevents me from getting what I want.

Overcoming anger (Cont.)

While it is undesirable to fail to get what I want, it is seldom awful or intolerable.

I can cope successfully with unfair people even though I strongly wish they would act better.

I wish others would treat me fairly but they never have to.

I do not need other people to act well – I only prefer it.

People act the way they do because that's the way they act. Tough!

I can live and be happy – though not as happy – with my significant other's fallibility.

My supervisor is fallible and will not always act fairly or competently. Tough – that's the way fallible human beings work!

I can put up with this negative and hostile person, though it would be better if he/she acted better.

In your Individual Action Plan, indicate the self-talk you can you use to overcome the blockers you have listed in Step 1. Take Stock.

Switch on the power of coping skills

There are powerful coping skills you can use to take control of your emotions and behaviour.

Find something fun to do

After an emotionally charged event, if you still find your emotional temperature running high – you might not be able to fly a kite to help distract or disengage yourself from the feelings you have, but you might be able to spend time with friends, listen to music or go for a brief walk. Consider some of the pleasant things available to you at work and after hours that can lower your emotional temperature.

Exercise

Do you exercise regularly? What time is available during your hectic day to exercise? Consider the multiple benefits of exercise. If you find it difficult to make the time to exercise, ask your friends or work colleagues how and when they find the time. Remember that top performers engage in regular exercise. Once you make the commitment to exercise, you will soon notice that it will be easier to do than you first thought.

Find Someone to Talk to

It's unhealthy to bottle up emotions. You may think it's uncool to talk to someone about issues you are having but it is very helpful if you can find someone you can trust to tell them how you honestly feel and to be able to explain the specific issues you are stressed about. When someone listens without initially offering advice, you can often figure out your next best move. You become more aware of any of the negative performance blockers you might be experiencing and you can then work on them.

Relaxation

In tough situations, do you attempt to keep your body calm? Do you consciously use specific techniques to stay relaxed such as slow deep breathing? The following instructions for the 5-3-5 breathing relaxation technique can guide your relaxation. You can use this technique as you prepare for a tough situation such as giving a public speech, meeting with someone who has a complaint about you or confronting your partner with a grievance.

This controlled, deep breathing technique can be used while sitting (or lying) down. To use this technique most effectively, you should employ deep breathing, beginning with your diaphragm and ending with the top of your lungs.

Here are some instructions on how to do it – take this opportunity to try it out.

To begin with, rapidly exhale all the air from your lungs.
Next, slowly to a count of five, inhale…one…two…three…four… five…
Hold your breath of air for a slow count of three…one…two…three…
Now slowly, very slowly, exhale the air to a slow count of five…one… two…three…four…five…

You have just completed one repetition. How do you feel?

To continue to relax, breathe in slowly again to a count of five, hold for a count of three, and again exhale to a slow count of five. After you have begun the exercise with an exhale to a count of five, all repetitions consist of counts of 5-3-5.

Solve the problem

An essential component of the high performing mindset is the ability to solve problems. Figuring out how to solve problems as quickly as possible is an asset. Of course, it helps if you are in a calm state of mind and body.

Here's a method many high performers use to solve problems. It is especially good for people who react impulsively to problems without first reflecting on the best way to handle the issue or situation. First, it helps to clearly identify what the problem is. Second, you come up with a number of different alternative solutions to the problem. Third, you weigh up the positive and negative consequences of each alternative. Fourth, once you have selected a preferred course of action, plan out the steps you will take and things you will say. Fifth, put the plan into effect. If it's successful, your emotional temperature should drop significantly. If it doesn't, try an alternative, don't give up.

Mindfulness

Mindfulness practice is learning to direct your attention to your experience as it is unfolding, moment by moment, with open-minded curiosity, being non-judgmental and accepting. It means focusing attention away from distracting internal thoughts and feelings and coming back to the present.

Mindful breathing is a popular technique to strengthen your attentional focus away from the negative.

Have someone read out loud the following instructions.

1. To begin, stand up, jump, stretch, turn, shake all your muscles out and then sit back down.
2. Sit comfortably, with your eyes closed and your back straight.
3. Bring your attention to your breathing. Imagine that you have a balloon in your tummy. Every time you breathe in, the balloon inflates or blows up. Each time you breathe out, the balloon deflates – the air is all let out. Notice how it feels in your tummy as the balloon fills up and goes down. Your tummy and your chest are rising with the in-breath and falling with the out-breath.
4. Continue to focus on your breathing. Thoughts will come into your mind, and that's okay, because that's just what the human mind does. Simply notice those thoughts that have gone for a wander and then bring your attention back to your breathing. This is how you make your brain strong.
5. Continue to focus on your breathing. You might notice sounds, smells or feelings but just bring your attention back to your breathing.

Open your eyes. How do you feel?

Be assertive

What is the best way to react to someone whose behaviour you want to change for the better?

There are three styles of conversation that you could employ only one of which may help you to achieve the results you want. Here are your options.

First, you can choose an *assertive* interpersonal style. You state clearly and directly what you are honestly feeling, thinking and wanting including the reasons why you still wish for the points to be included. You stick to the facts. You employ a confident, warm yet firm tone of voice. If you are having this conversation directly with the person, you have good eye contact. Your expression is relaxed, and you use your hands naturally.

Second, you can employ an *aggressive* interpersonal style. You use emotionally-loaded accusatory words and statements and you demand that your request be followed through. Your statements convey your superiority and the other person's inferiority. You blame and condemn them for what they have or haven't done. You threaten and insist they do as you say. Your tone of voice is sarcastic, tense, loud, icy and authoritarian. If you are face-to-face, your eyes are narrowed and cold. You stand with your hands on your hips, chest extended, fists and jaw clenched, and you appear tense.

Finally, you may elect to use a *passive* interpersonal style of communication. You never really say any more about what you want. You express yourself in a very rambling and disfluent style. You use apologetic words. In terms of your non-verbal behaviour, you express yourself faint-heartedly. Your voice is quiet and unsure. If you are discussing the issue in person, you avoid eye contact. You look downward, lean forward and stand well apart from the person you are addressing.

Using an assertive interpersonal style can strengthen your self-management because while you have expressed yourself and followed through with what you believe is correct, you do not alienate the other person by using the aggressive style. And while the passive style may be the less contentious, you will find you have achieved very little and are less likely to move forward to improve the situation. Consider which is your characteristic style when you are faced with interpersonal disagreements: are you typically assertive, aggressive or passive?

Gratitude
Be grateful for the good things that happen and do not focus on the bad things. The next time you are feeling negative about things, take a breath and focus on what you are grateful for both in your professional and private life. Make a mental list and even say it aloud. By shifting your focus from negative thoughts and their connected feelings, you will feel your mood change and energy increase. When colleagues or family members assist you with your work, communicate your appreciation.

Now, take a few minutes and focus on what you are grateful for. Share your thoughts with someone you care about or write down your thoughts. Keep a list of these "grateful for" items. Making a point of being consciously grateful every day for one or several things is a good start to improving your positive outlook on life.

Time Management

Having too much work to do and not enough time to do it – including taking work home with you and having it impinge on your home-family life – is a common causes of work stress for sure!

Boundary Ritual

A solid boundary between work and home enables you to recharge. A clear boundary helps you leave work at work, rather than dragging the stress of it home with you.

1. Set the intention to let go of your role at work.
2. Do something physical to help you release your work role.
3. Sync it up with your breath.

Imagine you arrive at home, come to a full stop and put the car into park. As you grab the keys before you remove them, set the intention and say: "I am going to exhale and remove the key to let go of my role at work." Inhale and remove the keys. Exhale letting go of your role at work. Release your job – go into your house.

The Schedule Hack

Do you carry a calendar at work? What's on it? Meetings? What else?

- Your spouse/partner's schedule?
- Your children's schedule?
- Your workout schedule?
- Your next date night?
- Some blocked off free time for yourself to be with friends, walk, bike, yoga, read a book, take a class?

Anything not on the calendar is not going to happen, period.

If you want to have a life, always carry your Life Calendar with you.

Step 1. Schedule your Life Calendar for the week ahead (other family members can do theirs as well). Enter these events on your weekly work schedule.

Step 2. Take a photo of your life calendar with your phone.

Step 3. Defend your Life Calendar (if someone asks you to do something extra, check your Life Calendar and be prepared to say "No, I have another commitment at that time"– not easy).

In your Individual Action Plan, indicate the coping skills you can you use to overcome the blockers you have listed in Step 1. Take Stock.

STEP 3: TAKE ACTION

Once you take control of your emotions and behaviour, you are ready for some actions to improve the situation and make the problem go away so that you can be stress-free and perform at your personal best!

As part of the mindset for high performance, four social and emotional skills are ready to be deployed: confidence, persistence, organisation and getting along.

I'll review each one now. See which you could use to deal with the tough situation you described in Step 1. Take Stock of your Individual Action Plan.

Be confident

When confronting problems that are challenging and with setbacks, use your best examples of verbal and non-verbal confident behaviour.

- Trying new things at the risk of failure
- In pressure situations, express my opinion
- Speaking with a clear, firm tone of voice when expressing my ideas
- Standing up for what you believe when others express a different opinion
- Standing up for someone who is being treated unfairly
- Beginning a project that no one else thinks is valuable, but you do
- Taking on a project that you don't know 100% about and to research it on your own
- Making suggestions to your superior about how to improve programming
- Volunteering to model good practices
- Asking for (and do not feel intimidated by) constructive criticism
- Standing up straight, tall with good body posture
- Taking opportunities to meet new people
- Maintaining eye contact

Persist!

When faced with time-consuming, boring tasks, gear up for the extra effort and avoid procrastination.

- Doing the work nobody wants to do but needs to be done
- Finishing unpleasant tasks early in the week
- Finishing all important tasks that have to be done
- Trying different approaches to master new technology

Get organised

When faced with time/work load pressures, get yourself organised.
- Keeping track of important meetings
- Planning the various steps to your project in advance to fit within time allocated
- Preparing for important meetings
- Setting deadlines to complete tasks
- Having proper equipment you need for lesson ready to go before lesson
- Having a file cabinet with filing system to file papers
- Writing down a list of what needs to get done each day
- Setting realistic goals and times by which they will be met
- Recording important meetings/events on a calendar
- Filling out a daily, hour-by-hour "what to do" chart

Get along

With everyone you come in contact with, work collaboratively, develop positive relationships, and communicate effectively.
- Avoiding gossip
- Providing constructive advice rather than give orders
- Making positive comments about colleagues
- Volunteering to work with others on projects
- Offering to help others
- Being a good listener
- Being flexible and not insisting it must be done my way
- Being open to learning new ideas from other people
- Relating positively to a difficult person

You might be thinking: If I'm not very confident or organised, how do I display these skills at work, home and in my life? The answer is to "Just do it", "Fake it till you make it" or "Face the fear" and do it anyway. The more you practice, the stronger you get.

To complete your Individual Action Plan, enter in Step 3. Take Action, those things you will do that apply one or more of the four social-emotional skills to get on top of the tough situation you described in Step 1. Take Stock.

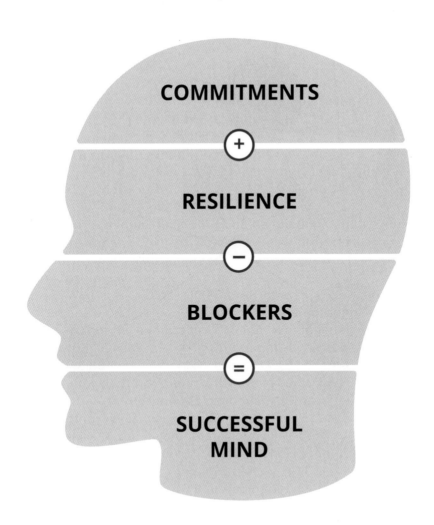

As you can see, strong COMMITMENTS and RESILIENCE are the dual aspects of a high performance mindset that enable you to cope in order to achieve your goals of success, positive relationships and wellbeing. In order to do your best job possible, resilience is required to survive the rigors and stresses of modern-day life. Without it, you are too vulnerable. With it, you are empowered.

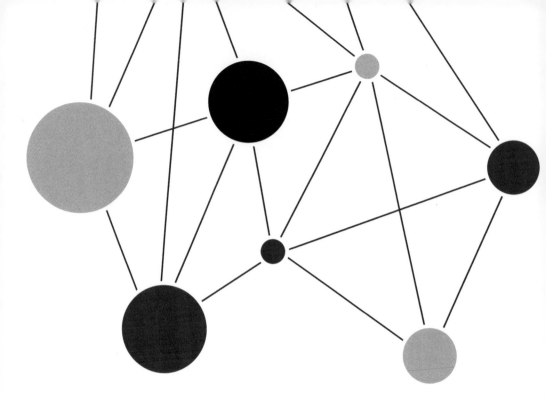

Part 5

Work

"Good thinking gets good results."
- Ed Nottingham, author, *It's Not as Bad as It Seems*

"The top flight executive is essentially logical and rational. At least, he better be. For although he is emotive, driving and behavior oriented in important ways, he is strong on thinking, imagining, planning and theorizing. He does not merely act, he uses his head. His greatest forte is that some individuals powerfully think, some heavily emote, and some pronouncedly act, he tends to engage in all three."
- Albert Ellis, author, *Executive Leadership: A Rational Approach*

"If you believe that you must get what you want, whatever the cost, you've put yourself into an emotional pressure cooker. We can partially attribute this rise in stress, anxiety, and depression to a negative and correctable style of thinking." Sam Klarreich, author, *Pressure Proofing. How to Increase Personal Effectiveness on the Job and Anywhere Else for that Matter*

"Rational beliefs bring us closer to getting good results in the real world."
- Albert Ellis, Founder, Rational Emotive Behavior Therapy

"Many employers have seen stressed-out, angry, frustrated or depressed colleagues and employees who have attitude problems. Employees carry these attitudes throughout their lives as well as to work and allow them to affect job relations and performances negatively, These characteristic attitudes and beliefs, therefore, should become the focus of learning and development workshops."
- Dom DiMattia, author, *Mind Over Myths*

STRENGTHENING HIGH PERFORMANCE MINDSETS

I've worked as a 'high performance' consultant and coach to organisations and individuals. I have focussed much of my work on helping people to become more aware of attitudes and ways of thinking that can either block or accelerate their journey towards success and happiness. I have strengthened the resilience of many to cope with the changes and challenges of work. I believe I have helped many become un-stuck at work discarding self-limiting beliefs, developing self-belief and the willingness to dream. I've learnt many things along the way that I want to share.

One of my first jobs as an organisational consultant was with the AMP (financial services) who asked me to develop a motivational program for middle-level insurance men and women. I created The Success Program that for many years became my blueprint for improving job performance which consisted of the following ingredients:

1. Dream big. Don't limit yourself by self-doubts, anxieties nor fear of failure. Commit to long-term success 100 per cent – whatever it takes. Clarify the value you place on achieving significant levels of job success. Choose and commit yourself to a long-term level of professional achievement while not limiting oneself by excessive anxieties that may arise from fear of failure.
2. Identify short-term and long-term professional goals (type of job, level of advancement, professional awards, significant contributions, professional skills and knowledge, financial).
3. Become aware of internal, personal obstacles to achieving these goals including indecisiveness, perfectionism, self-depreciation, procrastination and hostility towards others and see which will sabotage long-term success.
4. Consider as alternative to self-defeating attitudes that create internal obstacles alternative success-oriented, rational attitudes.
5. Develop an action plan whereby decisions are written down concerning where, when and how you will engage in those challenging behaviours which will help achieve various goals.

This program was so successful as appraised by participants and their senior-level direct reports that I was invited to develop a program for professional athletes at one of Australia's leading football clubs, Collingwood.

The focus of the program I developed for Collingwood was twofold. First, the sessions included specific success-oriented, stress managing mental skills and attitudes. Second, players identified stressful situations that had the potential for unsettling themselves and the team and strategies were discussed for handling these stressful situations during the week, immediately before and after a game.

Expectations of what players could expect from the program were realistic:

> 'What can you expect to get from the program? Because you are a team of individuals, your mental strengths and weaknesses differ quite a bit. I expect each of you will get something different from the program – ideas, skills. And because of the size of the group, it may be difficult to individualise how the material to be discussed applies to you. This mental training program will sensitise you to various aspects of your mental preparation and different mental skills so that after the session, you can work on those specific areas you would like to see improved.'

Forty players attended the program in groups of 10 for one hour per week before the season started. Here were the topics:

Week 1. Untapping of your mind and body.
Week 2. Programming your mind to take control of your body.
Week 3. Overcoming your fears and worries through winning attitudes and positive thinking.
Week 4. Setting goals: Your road to success.
Week 5: Improving your concentration.

Was the program a hit? Yes and no. While the program had full support of the coaching staff, it was nonetheless one of the first programs of its kind as it had a focus on what happens above the shoulders. This was a very new and novel concept for the players. Some of the old guard, more senior players, were sceptical throughout, while those younger players and for those who recognised the need for mental preparation, it was accepted. The benefits were certainly seen in an increase in the confidence and attentional focus of many players as well as an improved attitude towards the importance of training before games. Players became increasingly capable of setting and achieving higher and higher goals in different aspects of their playing – and goal production definitely increased for a few of the more inconsistent but highly talented players.

TAKING THE STRESS OUT OF TEACHING

MICHAEL E BERNARD

I was employed by our state Department of Education to work with groups of teachers who had taken leave of their work due to work stress. These were teachers of all ages, men and women, teaching at all levels of schooling. All were experiencing stress-related physical, emotional and psychological symptoms due to their work – and their doctors concurred they needed time out to recover and decide on whether to continue teaching. The central focus of my workshops attended by these teachers – who were all extremely passionate about their teaching and most wished to return – was the role their attitudes played in their stress. Why attitudes? Because, as a result of my work with individual teachers, I had discovered different unhealthy, stress creating attitudes and ways of thinking that increased their levels of stress.

These highly capable teachers were highly stressed in part because of their mindset. For example, they had a strong tendency to take adverse events at work personally (e.g., criticism, imperfect performance). Many added to their levels of stress by 'catastrophising' when faced with problems and difficult behaviour of their students, parents, senior school leaders or colleagues. These great teachers also made quite negative evaluations of time/ workload pressures (e.g., having to take work home). Additionally, many teachers were not comfortable talking about their stresses and strains of work to others, keeping emotions bottled; many believed they should be stronger to be able to cope.

I adapted the highly successful program for the insurance industry and sporting sector to the work of teachers. Central to the program was providing an insight into the internal causes of stressful emotions that highlighted the role of thinking and the choices teachers could make in restructuring their stress-creating self-talk, to stress-managing self-talk (ABCs of emotions).

Almost everyone who participated in the program that I offered over four years revealed through the surveys they completed on stress levels as benefitting a great deal. Many felt so inspired and motivated that they immediately put up their hands to return to teaching. Others decided that they should move on to other, less stressful occupations. (Make no mistake. Teaching is hugely stressful and as you probably know, many teachers retire early from teaching because of job stress.)

Over the years, the more I counselled and coached individuals of all ages, I could clearly see that their mindset was key in understanding why they experienced a great deal of job stress and why their work performance was not as positive as they wanted it to be. I was also seeing that when people were made aware of mindset, their inner CEOs, and were given and opportunity to learn about how their minds operate at their worst and best, they matured – as a good wine becomes great.

Today more than ever it is crystal clear to me that your mindset at work determines your destiny – as much if not more than the way your organisation operates and the personality of those you work for. Commitments to success, others and self along with strong resilience are the elements of a successful mind that develop across your work life.

In case you haven't done so already, you can give yourself a check-up from your neck-up by completing the high performance mindset survey on the next page.

HIGH PERFORMANCE MINDSET SURVEY

SELF-MANAGEMENT
When faced with tough situations, being aware of your emotions, staying calm, when upset, controlling one's behaviour, calming down and bouncing back.

☐

PERSISTENCE
Finishing tasks and activities that are frustrating, time consuming and/or boring with extra effort.

☐

ORGANISATION
Having a goal to be your best at work and knowing what to do to achieve it. Managing your time, energy and systems effectively.

☐

CONFIDENCE
Not being afraid to try something and not being worried about what others think. Speaking clearly with a confident voice.

☐

GETTING ALONG
Working well with others, treating others with respect, acceptance and resolve disagreements effectively.

☐

RESILIENCE

COMMITMENT SUCCESS

COMMITMENT OTHERS

COMMITMENT SELF

Instructions:

Rate the extent of development of each element of your mindset.

3

= highly developed very frequently reflected in my behaviour

2

= somewhat developed sometimes reflected in my behaviour

1

= needs further development infrequently reflected in my behaviour

BELIEFS

☐ **SELF DIRECTION**
Appreciating the importance of setting big goals at work; believing in the importance of confronting obstacles and solving problems without delay.

☐ **OPTIMISM**
Anticipating success; seeing bad events as temporary and good outcomes as being due to your ability.

☐ **GROWTH**
Believing that your ability and competence continues to develop from experience and ongoing learning.

☐ **CREATIVITY**
Believing in the importance of generating new solutions, ideas, or possibilities that may be useful in solving problems.

☐ **HIGH FRUSTRATION TOLERANCE**
Being prepared to endure frustration and difficulty in short-term in order to be successful in the long-term.

BELIEFS

☐ **ACCEPTANCE OF OTHERS**
Accepting that all people are fallible, mistake makers some of the time and not judging them by their behaviour.

☐ **EMPATHY**
Appreciating the importance of seeing the world from the eyes of another and being able to listen and tune into the feelings of others.

☐ **RESPECT**
Valuing others and appreciating the importance of treating people with consideration and care.

☐ **SUPPORT**
Valuing doing things that help others to be successful.

☐ **FEEDBACK**
Knowing the importance of providing others with information about how they have been performing their job for the purpose of improving individual and team performance.

BELIEFS

☐ **SELF ACCEPTANCE**
Accepting yourself as someone who is imperfect; not using your work performance or other's opinions to base your judgment of self-worth.

☐ **POSITIVE SELF REGARD**
Appreciating your strengths of character, personality, skills and ability as well as valuing positive aspects of your family, culture and religion.

☐ **AUTHENTICITY**
Believing in the importance of behaving consistently with your values and not having to go along with the group when their opinion differs from yours.

☐ **POSITIVE FOCUS**
Appreciating the positive rather than focusing on negative events and being grateful for what you have.

☐ **HEALTHY LIVING**
Believing in the importance of a healthy lifestyle including rest, recreation, relaxation and a balanced diet.

HIGH PERFORMANE PROBLEM SOLVING

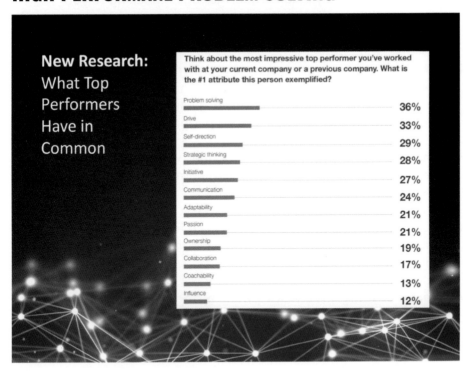

New Research:
What Top Performers Have in Common

Think about the most impressive top performer you've worked with at your current company or a previous company. What is the #1 attribute this person exemplified?

Problem solving	36%
Drive	33%
Self-direction	29%
Strategic thinking	28%
Initiative	27%
Communication	24%
Adaptability	21%
Passion	21%
Ownership	19%
Collaboration	17%
Coachability	13%
Influence	12%

What is a work problem? A work matter or situation regarded as unwelcome or harmful because it prevents you from achieving your goal and needs to be dealt with and overcome.

As the research shows no matter your commitment to succeed, to be great at what you do, you must be good at solving problems.

Now, the first thing to know is that there are two types of problems you can have at work (and life).

Practical problems. These problems are external to you, external circumstances – the tough situations that occur at work.

1. **Challenging work demands** (difficult tasks that may temporarily exceed your capacity to perform well; having to deliver a presentation to colleagues on a challenging topic; having to learn complex software; giving performance appraisals).

2. **Relationship difficulties** (being treated unfairly or unprofessionally by a colleague/manager speaking to you disrespectfully or who promises to complete a task that you need to have done but fails to follow through).

3. **Unproductive organisational practices** (little or no consultation/communication concerning decisions that affect you; re-organisation of your work responsibilities making it almost impossible for you to achieve your performance goals).

4. **Change** (rapid and significant changes with company re-structure, new responsibilities, new team to work with, new job location).

5. **Time/workload pressures** (too much to do, not enough time/support to do it; having to take work home; unrealistic deadlines; competing priorities).

6. **Receiving negative work performance evaluation** (negative feedback from someone whose opinion matters; not getting promoted; not getting bonus; not achieving monthly performance goals; quality of your team's output sub-standard).

Emotional Problems. These problems are your emotional and related behavioural responses to the practical problems. The stronger your emotional response to a practical problem, the harder it is to think clearly and behave effectively to solve the problem – or accept it if it doesn't go away.

1. **Anxiety** (fear of mistakes/failure; fear of disapproval/rejection).
2. **Feeling down and hopeless** (taking personally lack of success/disapproval).
3. **Anger** (the reaction to frustrating circumstances; unprofessional/unfair/disrespectful behaviour of others).

The various case studies presented so far in this book (Jimmy Chan, Gina Moriarity, Helen teacher-librarian, Jordie Blake) shine a light on how people's practical work-related problems, their emotional problems about their practical problems and their thinking makes a positive or negative contribution to the way they go about solving problems at work.

Consider the case of Jessie Hudson.

CASE STUDY.
JESSIE HUDSON,
FEMALE, 37 YEARS OF AGE

Jessie is a senior organisation development consultant for The City of Plankton, a growth corridor council in the north west of Melbourne. Stylish and popular, Jessie is the consummate professional who works hard, plays hard and reaps the benefits. Self-confident and assured in her interactions with the senior management team, she had a high profile at Plankton and was scaling her way up the career ladder when something rather unexpected happened and Jessie discovered that she was pregnant.

Jessie continued to work at Council throughout her pregnancy and negotiated some maternity leave for the period immediately following the birth of her child. Supremely confident in her ability, she honestly believed that she could seamlessly slip back into her role at Plankton and resume her career and her hectic work schedule whilst caring for her new baby.

When the baby hit the six month mark, Jessie was required to return to full time work and had booked her daughter into a council run childcare centre. Initially, Jessie's re-entry to the workplace had gone relatively smoothly. She had a training 'needs analysis' to complete, contracts to coordinate and bits and pieces of professional development to deliver. She cruised along for the first few weeks, but then the pressure had started to build. A sick child meant time away, sleepless nights spent feeding a restless infant made for slow starts to the day.

Jessie felt herself starting to struggle with the balancing act of being a mother and a full time learning and development guru. She felt her confidence ebbing away. Yes she was tired all the time and yes she looked a little less glamorous and yes there were niggling little voices in her head saying *'you are slipping...get a grip girl...you would not have done that ten months ago...you feel old...why doesn't anyone look at you anymore? Do they still think I can do the job?...I just don't care as much anymore...'*

And then the bombshell hit.

One month after returning to work Jessie had been called into Bill's, the Director of Corporate Services' office. Mark was looking a little uncomfortable and worried. 'Take a seat Jessie, I have some news for you and I want to make you an offer. Moira is leaving and I want you to sit in the chair until we source someone to take over as Manager of Human Resources. We will pay you acting duties and I want you to hold the fort until I find a replacement. What do you think? I know you are just back and there is a new baby and it will be a lot to manage but you have the team leaders and frankly, we don't have anyone else at your level that can do it. I don't want any big changes I just want you to hold it all down. We need you on this one Jessie, take a day to think about it and get back to me.'

Jessie had thought about it. She had a good relationship with the executive, she knew the pressure of the job, but she also knew that she had a great team of colleagues whom she knew would rise to the occasion. And then there was the money – right now it would not go astray to have an extra few hundred every pay. She had got back to Bill with a 'yes' and assumed the role of Manager of Human Resources while they advertised for a candidate.

What she had not realised was how difficult it was going to be to find a replacement for Moira. Council outsourced the recruitment to a head hunting company and the word was that HR professionals were thin on the ground. Consequently, Jessie had sat in the hot seat for a total of six months and the pressure of acting in the role had taken its toll.

The executive finally appointed someone from state government who came in with a reputation as being a ruthless 'toe cutter' – someone who liked to wield the knife of power more like a butcher than a surgeon. Initially Jessie had been delighted to welcome Sharon and had been somewhat relieved to hand it all over and reassume her role as senior consultant but then it all rapidly went pear shaped.

During the formal hand over, Sharon had made it clear that Jessie was no longer running the show and that all decisions must now be made by Sharon. In addition, she had frozen her project budget and announced that Jessie was not to meet with any senior managers without Sharon being informed and present at such meetings. Jessie had been gobsmacked. 'How dare she treat me like this – who the hell does she think she is – how am I supposed to do my job when I *can't talk to the executive group and have no budget ? The bitch – on a power trip and I am the sacrificial lamb...'*

After one week of working with Sharon, Jessie had stomped into Mark's office to demand a reversal of the arrangements, but Mark had simply said, *'I chose her and she is the new manager Jessie, give her a chance...'*

Jessie was squirming with mortification – all her hard work, all of the stress she had managed, all she had done for the organisation and with a new baby – all devalued in just one meeting. Initially she had blamed herself, *'What's wrong with me? Why have they let me down like this – they must think I am useless, a complete loser...'*

Clearly, Jessie was fuming as well as feeling anxious and whether or not her feelings were justified by work circumstances beyond her control, Jessie was confronted with two problems that unless solved were bound to do her in: 1. Her emotional stress and 2. Her practical problem of how to deal with Sharon. Here's what she did.

Jessie contacted her old manager and mentor Moira who talked her through the situation. Predictably, Moira had laughed and accused her of letting her ego get in the way of her capacity to handle the situation. 'You are more than able to influence Sharon. First, you need to be tougher, don't let your emotions rule you – call on your resilience to calm yourself down so you can figure out the best way to deal with Sharon. Can you come up with three strategies to employ with Sharon – and we can look at the positive and negative consequences of you implementing each one?

Jessie identified three strategies she could employ with Sharon and had analysed the positives and negatives. She could focus on what Sharon was doing wrong and why. She could ask Sharon to canvass the executive team and ask them about her capacity to manage budgets and with a positive endorsement, assertively request that her budget be returned to her; or she could find a way to make having her budget back advantageous to Sharon. Having decided on the best she was now ready to put her case and influence her manager.

'I must put her at ease and open with a positive. Complement her on taking such a thorough approach to orienting to the role and providing strong leadership . I will show her the force field analysis I have

completed and why having my own budget back will make her life easier. I have designed a same day report back process so she will be in the loop at all times...If I don't have a budget she will have to waste so much time checking and authorising – this way I do all the work and she just signs off."

Sharon opens her door and Jessie smiles and thanks her for taking the time to meet. The two women sit at the round table in Sharon's office and Jessie delivers her pitch. To her surprise Sharon listens attentively and then agrees to the budget being reinstated. *'It is never easy to give up power Jessie, I have been waiting for you to come and see me and I am glad you have. Your analysis is thorough and you have presented an excellent argument. By the way, you did a great job keeping the branch together for so long...any advice for me?'*

For the first time in months, Jessie starts to relax.

Emotional problem solving

Far and away the most important thing I know about emotional self-management is this ABC model.

John

    A = made redundant after 10 years in the company
    B = 'I don't have the skills for this industry. This is the worst thing that could happen. I can't stand it. I am useless.'
    C = depression, heavy drinking, makes no real effort to secure new job

Jim

    A = made redundant after 10 years in the company
    B = 'I can use my redundancy payment to start my own business. This could be worse. I can cope. I won't take this personally. I still have many things about myself I am proud of.'
    C = very disappointed but not depressed, after a break begins his new business

What we have learnt (see Part 4. Resilience) about the way our brains operate is that everyone has two different ways they can think about the same adversity: 1. Thinking that is rigid, extreme, not sensible and untrue which leads to unhealthy and self-defeating emotional and behavioural reactions, and 2. Thinking that is flexible, moderate, sensible and objective which leads to healthy, self-enhancing reactions.

Consider the way John thinks about redundancy: 'This is the worst thing that could happen. I can't stand it. I am useless." None of these thoughts are sensible, true or helpful. These rigid, extreme thoughts are causing John's self-defeating reactions to redundancy.

Jim's thinking about redundancy is more flexible, moderate, sensible, objective and helpful: 'This could be worse. I can cope. I won't take this personally. I still have many things about myself I am proud of.'

Rather than blaming others or the world for how you react, taking responsibility for how you feel and behave is very empowering – and is an important principle underpinning the solving of one's own emotional reactions to practical problems.

Practical problem solving

Introducing D-CAP

High effectiveness problem solving

Several years ago, our small business was faced with a large practical problem. As a result of our success in solving this problem, I developed D-CAP, an advanced skillset for solving practical problems.

CASE STUDY. THE BERNARD GROUP TAKES ON A BANK

We decided to convert all our curricula programs for schools to an online, digital format that required the development of a Learning Management System (LMS) to host our programs. The developer of our LMS advised us to go with their existing bank (Bank A) for the credit card facility we needed for online sales. This would save considerable costs since they had already set up the functionality for credit cards with this Bank. We set up an account with Bank A and applied for a credit card facility. Not only was our application rejected but an explanation as to why it was refused was not provided (it was against policy). We then approached Bank B which instantly approved us; however, the cost of installing Bank B's credit facility for online sales was going to cost us $10k more than if we went with Bank A. After several weeks of stewing, my sense that we had been treated poorly increased. I was pretty angry. I went back to Bank A and sought to speak to someone further up their chain of command – their Melbourne Business Manager. Understanding our needs and agreeing with the merit of our application, he agreed to lodge an appeal. The internal appeal was subsequently rejected – again, with a refusal of explanation. I persevered and Googled the name of Bank A's National Manager for Business. I called and was put through to his Executive Assistant. I presented my case to her and was told she would look into it. The EA contacted Bank A's NSW/ACT General Manager for Small Business Enterprises who called me to say he would further investigate asking for all the details. Within 72 hours we received approval for a credit card facility from Bank A and saved $10k. And, the explanation for initial rejection was given – they thought we were a non-registered training organisation offering courses to educators in schools – they failed to understand our business.

Had I not solved the problem, we would have; a. Spent a further 10k to create the payment gateway for the LMS, and b. Wondered why we were rejected and worry how that could further impact our good standing in business.

Putting D-CAP to Work
How to solve your problems

In thinking about the practical and emotional issues we overcame when the odds were stacked against us, I reflected on what aspects of my problem solving mindset helped. I created the acronym, D-CAP to explain it to myself and others.

To learn about D-CAP, why not select one of your existing, larger work problems. Next, answer the following two questions:

- How determined are you to solve the problem?
- How determined do you have to be in order to solve difficult problems?

D = Determination

In my experience, you have to be 100% determined to solve large, practical work problems in order to be successful.

If you are not completely determined to solve the problem, you can increase your determination by clarifying or reminding yourself what you see as the 'moral purpose' for what you do at work – who will benefit from what you do? What is at the heart of what you do at work? Why did you choose to work at what you do? What do you stand for? If you are in a position of leadership, why did you choose to become a leader? How would you like to be remembered by others when you retire? How can you keep track of yourself – to remember your heart?

In the above example with banks, my moral (as opposed to financial) purpose was and is very clear: to benefit the lives of young people, their happiness, relationships and achievements. This moral purpose helps my determination to do everything I can to overcome obstacles and to endure what seems at times as endless frustrations.

Determination to solve problems is a constituent element of having a strong Commitment to Success as I discussed in Part 2 of this book.

C = Confidence

Even the most successful and high achieving amongst us can lack confidence.

Confidence is one of those 'take it for granted' traits that people think you're born with or you're not.

Confidence is a mindset. As such, it can be developed.

Confidence depends on your Resilience and your ability to manage anxiety. Anxiety blocks your confidence. It does for me. So, a key to being confident in solving problems is to accept that people may well not think highly of you if you take it upon yourself to confront them if they are part of the problem and solution – as I did in confronting management with confidence at Bank A in the above example.

Accept that you do not need people's approval, you can survive without it and that it's not the end of the world if people think you have a big head for wanting to see things turn in a way you believe in.

Confidence is the self-belief that you have what it takes to solve the problem. While I was not confident that I would be able to reverse Bank A's decision to approve our credit application, I was confident in tackling the problem – I knew that I was right.

What's your confidence 'trick' when faced with a difficult problem to solve?

Here's some strategies for strengthening confidence needed to solve problems.

1. Recognise that your past successes were due to your effort and talent and not due to luck or ease of task.
2. If lacking in confidence, 'fake it till you make it'.
3. Feel the fear and do it anyway.

4. Get rid of negative self-talk.
   'This is too hard.'
   'If I wait long enough, the problem will go away.'
   'I'll solve this problem when I am in the mood to do so.'
   'I'm not smart enough.'
5. Talk up your confidence with positive self-talk.
   'I've done hard things before, I can solve this difficult problem.'
   'I have the talent and experience to solve difficult problems.'
   'I am smarter than I think.'

A = Action

One of my favourite expressions is '"Do, don't stew' and this applies to solving problems. Taking action does not mean, however, flying off the handle to try to solve the problem. Think first, don't react. Think of alternative solutions to the problem – the positive and negative consequences of each – and pick the one that seems best; just like Jessie Hudson did before she approached Sharon to assume control of her budget.

Assertive action is frequently required to solve problems. Assertiveness stands between aggression and passivity and involves communicating in a polite but firm manner what you are thinking, feeling and wanting.

'I am thinking that my small business is being treated unfairly and disrespectfully by your Bank (A). For no apparent reasons that you have shared with us, you have rejected our application. I am feeling very cross and hard done by. I would like you to reconsider your decision and that is why I am taking my case to the highest level of bank leadership. Thank you.'

Effective action also requires careful planning of what you plan to say and do and creation of a timeline.

Evaluate the impact of your plan, go again if not successful at first and be prepared to go to Plan B.

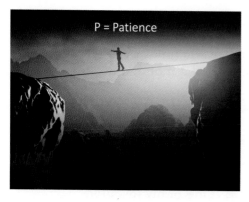

P = Patience

Patience means the capacity to accept or tolerate problems without becoming highly annoyed or anxious. Many problems take a while to fix. Some problems require a different time and context before change is possible. How patient are you when faced with challenging people and problems to solve?

There are some problems that before they can be solved require significant change in who you are working with or for – or in the way your organisation operates. Therefore, when a problem does not seem solvable at the moment, keep the problem somewhere on your radar screen knowing that when circumstances change and with the passage of time, you will take further action. I am by nature very impatient. I want things done now. I have learnt that by being impatient for problems to be solved immediately, I am at a disadvantage.

Support

Know when it's time to seek advice. Your social capital – the network of colleagues and contacts to call on to – can help with identifying a solution. When you find yourself growing too impatient to handle a particular situation or solve a problem, seek advice from a mentor or another trusted resource who can add value and provide you with needed perspective.

Be sure to pick the right person. Here, you are not looking for emotional support as much as you are looking for someone to add his/her intelligence, experience and knowledge of you to point you in a different direction to solve the problem. Do not be afraid to reach out. It will be a privilege for the person you contact to help. Don't forget, this road runs in both directions. So, when faced with a tough situations, separate the practical from the emotional. Clearly define each. With a high performance mindset, you will have available solutions for each.

OVERCOME FEAR OF FAILURE, INDECISIVENESS AND PERFECTIONISM

I worked with Mary, the owner of a very successful restaurant, who was complaining that over the past few years she had missed out on business opportunities because she was overly cautious in committing her money. 'I had the money to spend and if I had, I'd have made a packet and been able to move on to new and more exciting projects. Instead, I waited until I was totally sure of getting my money back and by that time, it was too late.'

Indecisiveness is a type of procrastination, which is often motivated by a fear of failure. In discussing this relationship with Mary, she became aware that for as long as she could remember, she was very conservative when it came to making business decisions and the thing she feared the most when faced with a decision was not the actual loss of money but rather that she would make a mistake. Fear of mistake-making can disrupt your natural journey towards trying out and accomplishing more difficult and challenging tasks which, when achieved, would bring you intrinsic satisfaction.

The fear of making mistakes acts as a negative force diverting you from things you know deep within yourself you would be best to take on. So why did Mary fear failure? It will come as no surprise that the reason has to do with thoughts about completing the task. There are three particular ones, which lead to high anxiety. Let's deal with them one at a time.

'I must be successful all the time in everything important that I do.'

Now on the face of it, this idea seems reasonable. Aren't you supposed to strive hard for success? Yes, indeed! The trap in the above idea is in the word 'must'. It is, for the reasons discussed above, quite sensible to desire and strongly prefer success. However, when you take that rational strong desire and convert it into a demand of having to be successful all the time, then you are setting yourself up for high levels of anxiety. What the above attitude often does is place too much pressure on yourself to be successful. The notion that you must be successful all the time further increases your anxiety because you know from past experience that it is only a matter of time before you make a mistake (all humans are mistake-makers some of the time).

So the above attitude starts to generate high anxiety and can result in avoidance. If you endorse such a belief, ask yourself the question: 'Where is it written that I **must** be successful all the time? Is there a law of the Universe which says that I have to always be successful and never make a mistake?' Of course, when you look at it rationally, there is plenty of evidence of people encouraging us to be successful, but no one really assumes that it is possible for anyone to always be successful.

'It is terrible to not be achieving and make mistakes.'

The more you believe that making mistakes at things you set out to do is horrible and terrible, some kind of real catastrophe, the more likely you will be to experience high anxiety and, therefore, either perform the task poorly or procrastinate at getting around to doing the task. Mary literally creates her anxiety by telling herself how totally bad it would be for her to make a mistake or not be successful. To help people like Mary modify 'awfulising' about not doing well or making mistakes, I ask: 'Compared to becoming permanently paralysed, having a heart attack, having someone in your immediate family suffering an incurable disease, your house burning down, getting fired or going bankrupt, how bad is making a mistake in this particular situation?' I further point out that the words terrible and awful mean 100 per cent bad or worse and ask whether that's how they would evaluate making a mistake.

'To make a mistake or fail would make me a failure.'

In equating your total self-worth with your performance, you are putting your ego on the line every time you set out to achieve something and by so doing, you imbue the task with unhealthy anxiety. And given the belief that you **must** do well, and that if you don't you're no good, it is better to procrastinate and do nothing than to risk the possibility of failure and finding out that you are worthless. Learning to accept yourself with your imperfections is a key attitude to overcoming procrastination.

Diagnosis

Perfectionism

Now 'perfectionism' is an extreme form of fear of failure. Not only must you be successful in what you set out to do, you must do it perfectly. There is nothing wrong with striving to be perfect although I'm not convinced that setting an unrealistic goal for yourself is going to bring out the best in you. Why unrealistic? Because no matter how smart and talented you are, there will be times and areas of your work in which you will not achieve perfectly. However, the factor which leads to your anxiety and task avoidance is that you **demand** that you perform perfectly.

It is not easy to give up your perfectionism. You have grown up and got to where you are today believing that 'perfectionistic' attitudes towards your work helps you achieve what you want and brings out the best in you. When you were younger, perfectionism probably was a good psychological insurance policy in that it helped you, up to a point, perform well and possibly feel secure within yourself. The question you could ask yourself is whether perfectionism is still getting you what you want. Does insisting on doing tasks perfectly help you achieve what you want? Do you have excessive anxiety, which interferes with your performance because of your need to be perfect? And does high anxiety ever lead you to delay doing or finishing things which are not perfect?

If you are a perfectionist, try to see clearly that it is sometimes good to perform less than perfectly. On certain occasions, by finishing tasks which are less than perfect – but good enough to get by – you will find more time to concentrate on other tasks. Moreover, performing less than perfectly will help you discover what you can and cannot do, thus enabling you to focus your attention on your areas of strength. Much important learning and self-discovery takes place through 'trial-and-error' learning. To not permit yourself to err is to deny yourself vital information about yourself.

The following steps combat perfectionism.

1. Acknowledge your anxiety. Don't try to deny it.
2. Accept that anxiety is part of the human condition.
3. Accept responsibility for making yourself anxious. Don't blame your environment or your parents. After all, as I've shown, it is your own attitudes which largely determine your degree of anxiety.
4. Recognise that although anxiety is bad because its uncomfortable, it is not terrible and can be tolerated.
5. Work hard at accepting yourself even with your anxiety and convince yourself that while anxiety is bad, you are not bad.
6. Dispute with yourself the belief you have that you must perform perfectly all the time. Give up totally unrealistic standards you may have for yourself as well as your demands that your standards must always be achieved.

PROCRASTINATE LATER!

While I wrote about procrastination as a major blocker to positive performance in Part 4, I want to drill down a bit more into this perplexing behaviour – perplexing because even though we see the disadvantages in putting off doing something important at work, we do it anyway.

I want to emphasise right from the start that everyone procrastinates. It doesn't matter if you are the chief executive officer of a huge international organisation, publisher of a major book company, bus driver, hairdresser, real estate agent, student, housewife or househusband. It doesn't matter if you are rich or poor, young or old, white, black or any other colour. People from all backgrounds, experiences and ages procrastinate.

Common excuses for procrastination

Some people find it hard to admit to themselves they are procrastinating. Instead, they make up what are called 'rationalisations' which are reasons that are superficially acceptable to explain why they are putting off doing something important. Here are the most common excuses.

'I do not have time to do this today. It will be easier for me to do it tomorrow.'

'I'll do it as soon as other things in my life have cleared up."

'Make hay while the sun shines.'

'Since I do my best work under pressure, I'll just postpone this until the pressure builds.'

'Once before I did something just before deadline and it worked out well; I'll do it at the last minute again.'

'If I wait until the last minute to complete my work, I'll save myself lots of time and effort.'

'There's no point in starting if I don't know how to do the job properly.'

'I really don't want to do this anyway.'

If you want to reduce procrastination, you have to start by admitting you procrastinate – and then rip up any of these excuses for why you are.

The next step is to explore the 'real' reasons for your procrastination.

When I procrastinate, I have something I want to do but as I get started, I feel there are invisible forces that block me or pull me away from getting the job done. I created 'the magnetic theory of procrastination' to explain my procrastination and help me identify the reasons for when I put off doing important things.

The 'real' reasons we procrastinate

You can see from the accompanying drawing that there are 10 reasons I've identified why people procrastinate. You can see that there is a large black arrow under each reasons that indicates a force field that blocks you from the task you want to accomplish. There is one reason, 'immediate pleasure-seeking', that has an upward arrow showing that there is a force field that pulls you away from doing the task you've set out to do.

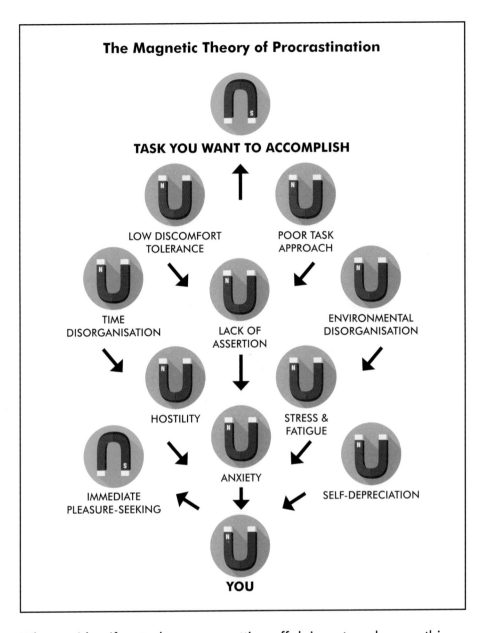

The Magnetic Theory of Procrastination

TASK YOU WANT TO ACCOMPLISH

LOW DISCOMFORT
TOLERANCE

POOR TASK
APPROACH

TIME
DISORGANISATION

LACK OF
ASSERTION

ENVIRONMENTAL
DISORGANISATION

HOSTILITY

STRESS &
FATIGUE

IMMEDIATE
PLEASURE-SEEKING

ANXIETY

SELF-DEPRECIATION

YOU

Why not identify a task you are putting off doing at work, something that really should be done. Then see if you can pick the reasons for your procrastination from the drawing above. Maybe you are feeling anxious, worried about what people will think if you don't perform the task at a good enough standard. Perhaps you are hostile about having to do the task. Maybe the level of discomfort and frustration in performing the task is more that you can take. Or it might be that you are simply doing other things at work that are more fun, immediately pleasureable, leaving little time or energy to perform the task you are putting off.

BEING 'AT CAUSE' OR 'BEING AT EFFECT'

A friend and colleague of mine, Russ Grieger, shared with me an important idea about the belief system of people. Russ says that some people believe they have no choice but to respond to outside events; they are 'at effect' – meaning that they are easily effected and distracted by outside events in their lives. These individuals tend to be a bit passive, do not like to take risks and believe things just happen to them.

In the case of procrastination, as they walk towards engaging with an important task to be done at work, they allow themselves to be pulled off course – as though someone is pulling one of their their earlobes – by outside forces like environmental disorganisation and inside forces like their anxiety or self-depreciation.

Other people are 'at cause' means they do everything they can to control their destiny. When they have a task that needs doing, they do not allow themselves to be pulled off course – no matter how strong the tug is on an earlobe to stop them from working or to move to something fun to do.

As much as I can, I try to 'be at cause' rather than 'at effect' so that when I feel something tugging at me, blocking me from engaging with and completing tasks that can be difficult or very frustrating and time-consuming, I remain strong, determined to get the job done – no matter the forces that are operating against me.

COACHING

High performance mindset coaching has a focus on helping people become aware of the strengths of their commitments to success, others and self as well as their resilience in order to achieve those work goals they have set for themselves. Central to high performance mindset coaching is helping people become aware of their performance blockers, the aspects of their thinking that are unhelpful and helping people to modify the way they think about what happens at work.

Here are two case studies that highlight different tough situations where high performance mindset coaching can help.

CASE STUDY. JOHN WARREN

John is a graduate trainee with a State Government agency. He has been working in the human resources unit for three months with a number of mature-age and very experienced personnel managers. Although generally talkative and socially friendly, he seems reluctant to actively participate in staff meetings and to make comments in interviews he has attended. He doesn't want to appear to be asking silly questions so generally remains silent. Recently, he was given the task of constructing a psychological profile proforma for new employees but feels like he doesn't know enough about this area and doesn't want to seek help so early in his tenure.

CASE STUDY. FRED FARNSWORTH

Fred has recently been promoted to a middle management position after 10 years as a key shop floor operative. Although he actively sought out this position he now finds himself dealing with and being responsible for a whole new range of issues. This includes mundane paperwork and 'administrivia', which he finds unsatisfying. He is missing report date deadlines and spending more and more time back on the shop floor where he feels more comfortable. Although his new position is more prestigious with better pay and more benefits, Fred feels he needs to return to the shop floor after only two months in his new position.

COACHING SUGGESTIONS FOR HANDLING TOUGH WORK SITUATIONS

Tough situation 1. Speaking in public on something the coachee doesn't know a lot about or has not spoken on before.
Coaching Suggestion: Prepare yourself by being relaxed (self-management) and confident. Be optimistic that your talk will go OK; don't worry about making a mistake – just continue on – it doesn't have to be perfect.

Tough situation 2. Coachee makes significant mistakes (e.g. underestimating budget).
Coaching Suggestion: Don't take it personally. It's bad but not the worst thing that could happen. I'm sure you have learned something from the experience so that it won't happen again.

Tough situation 3. There are complaints about the coachee from someone outside his organisation he works with.
Coaching Suggestion: I understand that you would be upset. However, what I've learned is not to take complaints personally. I remind myself that while I prefer people to think well of me, I don't need them always to be positive and that it's not the end of the world to be criticised. In fact, it's quite normal and expected. I try to see what I can learn from what they are saying to improve my job performance.

Tough situation 4. Coachee has overlapping projects and multiple deadlines that she may not be able to meet.
Coaching Suggestion: Get organised. Write down each project and when the project is due. Then, work out what steps you will need to take to complete the project and how long each step will take. See if you can get an extension – also, see if someone is around that can give you a hand.

Tough situation 5. A client is continually negative towards the coachee and is unfairly critical.
Coaching Suggestion: Expect that some people will be that way. Don't take it personally. Be confident. Use getting along skills to see if you can get them on your side. Be assertive in expressing what you think without being defensive or aggressive.

CASE STUDY OF HPMW COACHING: MANAGER FACES A DIFFICULT GENERAL MANAGER

The following interchange took place after two coaching sessions with a manager, Peter Wilson, who took advantage of coaching services provided to employees of his company. In the first two coaching sessions, time was spent on discussing *Peter's Commitment to Self*. During these sessions, Peter indicated that he wanted to work on strengthening *self-acceptance* and having a *positive focus*. During the first sessions, time was spent discussing tough situations that arose where Peter wished to be more self-accepting with examples of self-accepting, self-talk being reviewed and Peter reminding himself not to put himself down when members of his team seemed apathetic or dismissive of his ideas.

In terms of developing a more positive focus, I suggested Peter keep a record at the end of each day of three things that occurred during the day that he appreciated, that may have helped him, and which he was grateful for (Gratitude Record).

Peter decided he also needed to strengthen his Commitment to Others including *empathy*. To begin, he agreed to do a lot more listening and a lot less advice giving to those on his team.

At the beginning of coaching session three, Peter arrived wanting to discuss a problem he was having with his General Manager.

Michael:	So, how's your week been?
Peter:	Generally speaking, pretty good. I'm paying more attention to what is going well during my day rather than what isn't. In meetings with my team, I start off by what we discussed last week – shedding light on what's right and being more public in my recognition and appreciation of an individual's performance.
Michael:	So increased positivity is paying off?
Peter:	I feel more upbeat about dealing with things and there seems to be a lot more talking and energy at our meetings.
Michael:	Any situations come up that you'd like to discuss?
Peter:	There is an issue with one of our General Managers, Jane, that's pissing me off.

Michael: So I understand, what's her position and relationship to you?

Peter: Sure. I'm manager of the creative division of our company. She has the first and final say over whether new projects I propose get support and funded.

Michael: I see. Can you describe what happened the last time you were pissed off?

Peter: OK. This is fairly typical. At our last meeting, when we discussed forward planning, I put forward the view that we should move somewhat beyond our target market and develop something for a younger population that I thought I could adapt from some of the very successful IP I developed two years ago.

Michael: What did she say?

Peter: She shut it down. She said that the younger population was not our core business and that we couldn't be successful in marketing this new product. Furthermore – and this really got me angry – she made up a story as far as I can tell that she overheard a conversation at a recent sales conference between two people who work for our competitor who said that they had lost a lot of money in their latest efforts to diversify into the younger market with a similar product I wanted to develop. Jane has a habit of inventing stories to support her positions.

Michael: So, how did you respond to that tough situation?

Peter: I got into an argument telling her the reasons why my idea was a good one. She really didn't listen to me. Bad tone of mine I guess. Then I didn't really say anything. I just fumed and have stayed well away from her. I haven't spoken to her since the meeting.

Michael: Just to make sure I've got the picture, when you put forward a proposal to develop a new product for a new market, your manager shut it down and appeared to make up a story to justify the reason for her negative response. You got very angry and since then you have not communicated with her.

Peter: That's about it.

Michael: I can imagine that her behaviour affected you this way, I would be very frustrated too, if the situation happened to me.

Peter: This is not the first time this has happened. She seems to be on a power trip and if she hasn't thought of the idea, or if the idea puts her outside her comfort zone, like having to do more work – or if the idea originates with me – she just says 'No'. Basically, I've written her off and will have nothing to do with her.

Michael: We should probably look at the way you have been responding to Jane's negativity and see if it is helping you get what you want.

Peter: How do you mean?

Michael: For a minute, let's put aside her clearly negative behaviour towards you when you discuss new projects. Let's consider whether your anger and avoidance of her is helping you to achieve what you want.

Peter: Well, it isn't really. Jane rarely offers me any support for anything I do and doesn't pass on emails that she used to that have importance to me. We definitely have a conflicted relationship you might say.

Michael: OK. Again, setting her behaviour aside, what would the impact on her attitude towards you be if you were calmer when she responded negatively towards you – and if, at other times, you use your well-developed getting along skills to see if can get her on your side?

Peter: Why would I want to do that? She's at fault, not me – why should I have to change?

Michael: You don't. But you've just said that your conflicted relationship with her is making life worse for you as she is less supportive and doesn't share important information with you.

Peter: I can see what you are saying. Maybe I need to change my thinking and behaviour without expecting her to change first.

Michael: Makes sense. When is your next meeting?

Peter: This coming Tuesday I think.

Michael: Why not set a goal for how you could respond more positively if at Tuesday's meeting she is, again, negative to your ideas. How would you like to feel and respond if she makes a negative comment?

Peter: I'd like to feel less angry, calmer and be more confident and assertive without being hostile in the way I respond.

Michael: Sounds OK to me. To prepare for the meeting, is there any realistic self-talk you could use to prepare for the meeting and you can use if she makes a negative comment?

Peter: Positive self-talk? I could think: 'I don't have to let her get me angry. I am the boss over the way I feel even when she behaves so negatively. Negative comments are bad but not the end of the world and I can cope with them.'

Michael: Are you sure you can stand her negative behaviour?

Peter: I guess.

Michael: Remind yourself that you can stand just about anything that life dishes out to you by making up your mind to do so.

Peter: Yeah, I get that.

Michael: Any coping skills that can help you stay calm if you are being provoked?

Peter: I can relax more – take a few breaths.

Michael: If you consider using your behavioural strengths, are there any that you need to bring to play to see if you can tip the relationship back to at least a neutral one?

Peter: Yeah, getting along. I can find some time when she seems relaxed to discuss things other than work – and throwing her a few compliments wouldn't hurt.

Michael: Wouldn't hurt you?

Peter: Wouldn't hurt anyone.

While there is no guarantee that the plan Peter constructed with my coaching support would result in an immediate improvement or change in his General Manager's behaviour, it was the case that Peter was highly successful in becoming much more self-managing in staying calm when dealing with his GM. He also displayed much more positive behaviour that is now having the effect of returning peace to the relationship – at least for the moment.

PETER WILSON'S INDIVIDUAL ACTION PLAN. HIGH PERFORMANCE MINDSET

I. Strengthening Commitments

a. Which commitment do you wish to focus on and develop over the next few weeks? Which of the following beliefs will you put into practice on a regular basis to develop the commitment?

☐ Commitment to Success   ☑ Commitment to Others   ☑ Commitment to Self

☐ Self-Direction	☑ Acceptance of Others	☐ Authenticity
☐ Optimism	☑ Empathy	☑ Self-Acceptance
☐ Growth	☑ Respect	☑ Positive Focus
☐ High Frustration Tolerance	☑ Support	☐ Positive Self-Regard
☐ Creativity	☐ Feedback	☐ Healthy Living

b. What are the actions you will take at work to put the belief(s) into practice?

positive focus + feedback: Record three positive behaviours of others on my team and express appreciation

empathy: Listen without interrupting or expressing my opinion

acceptance of others: Not being so hard on team members who do the wrong thing — focus on their behaviour, watch my negative non-verbals

c. Record in the space below any observations about how well you were able to act on the belief(s) at work. Did you observe any benefit? What changes will you need to make to more effectively or regularly action the belief(s)?

positive focus + feedback: Good, feel better about my leadership and our team

empathy: Easier to do than I thought

acceptance of others: Still intolerant and I show it

II. Strengthening Resilience

What follows is a three-step model that you can use to plan positive and effective ways to tackle tough situations.

Step 1: Take Stock

Step 1 is designed to help you to focus on a specific situation, your personal reactions that make it harder to perform positively and to enable you to set a goal for the way in which you would like to manage the situation the next time it occurs.

a. Write down with some concrete detail (who, what happened, when, where) a 'significant' tough situation at work where you experience one or more of the four performance blockers at high intensity and where your work performance suffers. You can review the results of your Inventory of Tough Situations.

Tough Situation: My GM is very negative and unsupportive of me at meetings

The work situation is an example of which of the following types?

- ☐ Challenging work demand
- ☑ Relationship difficulty
- ☐ Unproductive organisational practice
- ☐ Change
- ☐ Receiving negative work evaluation

Other: _____

_____

b. Which performance blockers (negative emotional and behavioural responses) do you need to eliminate?

- ☑ Strong anger towards another
- ☑ Excessive worry about the future, my performance, what others think
- ☐ Feeling very down about my work performance and/or what someone thinks
- ☐ Procrastination at doing things I know are important to do

Other: _____

_____

c. Goal setting. Select from the following list the positive ways you would like to feel and behave the next time you are confronted with the tough situation.

- ☑ Calm
- ☑ Confident
- ☑ Hopeful
- ☑ Energetic

- ☑ Relaxed
- ☑ Positive
- ☐ Assertive
- ☐ Determined

Step 2. Take Control

In Step 2, you will have an opportunity to use and further develop your behavioural strength of Self-Management to stay calm or calm down before you tackle the situation at hand.

a. What examples of rational, positive self-talk can you use to be self-managing of your emotional reactions?

- ☑ 'This situation is bad but not awful.'
- ☑ 'I've done hard things like this before, I can do this.'
- ☑ 'I can stand this situation even though I don't like it.'
- ☑ 'I won't judge this person by his/her behaviour.'
- ☑ 'I accept myself no matter what.'
- ☐ 'I'll do the best I can.'

Other examples of rational, positive self-talk you can use:
Getting pissed off only makes things worse — better figure out another way to make her less negative.

b. Which coping skills will you use to self-manage in order to stay calm or calm down?

- ☑ Find someone to talk to
- ☐ Find something fun to do
- ☑ Figure out how to solve the problem
- ☐ Time management

- ☑ Relax
- ☐ Exercise
- ☐ Be assertive
- ☐ Be grateful

Other coping skills you will use to self-manage emotions:
Stop obsessing

Step 3. Take Action

In Step 3, you will want to decide which social-emotional skills you can use to tackle the situation and go one better including writing down the specific actions you will take.

a. List one or more ways to handle the situation. Consider positive and negative consequences of each and select one with the greatest likelihood of success.

Talk with GM seeking feedback

Wait it out before reacting

Identify what triggers her negativity towards me and avoid these triggers

b. Which social-emotional skills will you use the next time the tough situation arises to solve the problem and go one better?

☑ Confidence   ☑ Persistence
☑ Organisation   ☑ Getting along

c. Concretely describe how you will behave the next time you are faced with the tough situation.

calmly say how the decision not to support a new project in my department is effecting long-term growth and profitability — say in a polite way can she re-consider and, maybe, we can work on this together to find a way to do this.

d. Reflective comments on how you approached the situation, the success of your plan and any further changes you will need to make in your approach to the tough situation.

GM seems more receptive but still I'm finding it hard going; I am calmer — maybe go for lunch?

LEARNING AND DEVELOPMENT

No matter the state of the economy and a business' bottom line, there is always a tussle in deciding where to spend money on professional development. While there is agreement that in today's world, people have to do more with less and that there is a general perception of talent insufficiency, there still is an inclination to invest L&D dollars in skillset rather than mindset. Here's what I think.

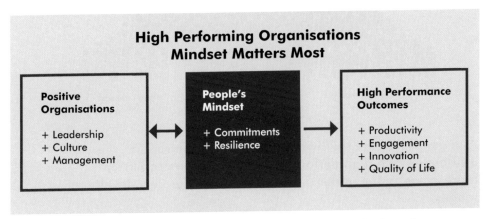

The collective mindset of people determines the level of performance of individuals in an organisation and overall performance outcomes of the organisation.

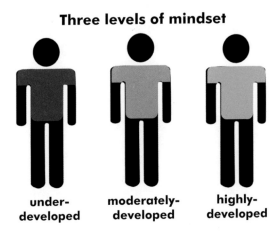

We know that in a team or across a whole department or organisation, employees at all levels bring with them different degrees of development of a high performance mindset.

Distribution of People's High Performance Capabilities in Low Performing Organisations

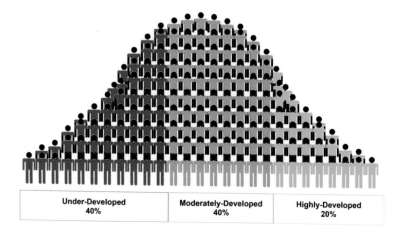

Under-Developed 40%	Moderately-Developed 40%	Highly-Developed 20%

As a generalisation, in lower performing organisations, the distribution of a high performance mindset is more highly represented in the under-developed and moderately developed ranges.

Consider under-developed work performance mindsets as the 'hidden cause' of talent insufficiency.

Distribution of People's High Performance Capabilities in High Performing Organisations

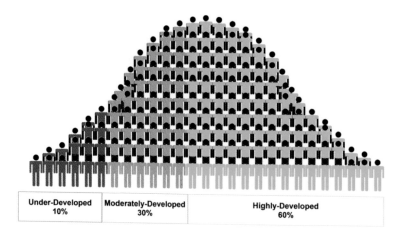

Under-Developed 10%	Moderately-Developed 30%	Highly-Developed 60%

Without question, leaders, managers and by downward extension employees of better performing organisations have more highly developed commitments to success, others and self as well as resilience.

An organisation's competitive advantage is found in the proportion of its leaders and managers who demonstrate a high performance mindset at work.

Food for thought

Shifting the distribution of a high performance mindset of leaders, managers (and employees) has a very large impact on individual, team and organisational performance.

What follows are several case studies where high performance mindset training was directed at reducing stress and improving work performance – with very positive outcomes.

Monash**Health**

Licences the *High Performance Mindset at Work* for 13,000 employees!

Monash Health is the largest public health service provider in Victoria servicing more than a million episodes of health care a year.

In 2013, Organisational Development & Learning (Human Resources) at Monash Health entered into an agreement with The Bernard Group to make the High Performance Mindset at Work program available to its 13,000 employees.

In order to maximise flexibility of access and widespread utilisation, Monash Health licensed the HPMW eLearning program for all its employees. Unique and confidential usernames and passwords are provided to each participating employee.

Monash Health has a long-standing tradition of providing learning and development support for employees. It viewed the *High Performance Mindset at Work* program as helping support its employees with the self-management and resilience needed for employees at all levels to continue to provide Monash Health's high standard of care.

The impact of HPMW has been evident.

Monash Health's Manager of Organisational Development & Learning writes on the benefits for employees who have completed the HPMW program.

'Introducing the High Performance Mindset at Work as an online resource has allowed us to provide education and support to our fantastic teams across the organisation. With over 13,000 employees and 42 sites that include five major hospitals in the region, this program has allowed us to get the key principles of building resilience across in a consistent way that is supported by research evidence. We have encouraged a team-based approach to the HPMW course where colleagues come together in reflective practice sessions to discuss their online learning experiences and identify different strategies for looking after themselves and their colleagues as they bring a high performance mindset to deliver the best outcomes for our patients.

'So far, over 470 employees including members of my own team have engaged with the HPMW program. The feedback has been very encouraging with many comments about the practical value of the course content and the convenience of having it available online.'

CASE STUDY: CRISIS INTERVENTION AT A HOSPITAL. SENIOR LEADERSHIP RESILIENCE

Case description. A major health care provider in Melbourne providing services to a significant population was experiencing a challenging situation that needed external professional support and assistance to provide crisis intervention.

Reason for Michael Bernard being engaged. The CEO requested help to support a senior executive-level, leadership team to deal with issues surrounding a very intense conflict between staff, senior medical leadership and the union. As a result, according to the CEO, the 'crisis' was having a detrimental effect on the health and performance of members of the hospital's senior leadership team. Each member of the leadership team experienced a loss of their natural resilience including the ability to self-manage their emotions.

Through consultation with the CEO, it was agreed that Michael Bernard would offer the *High Performance Mindset at Work – Resilience Program for Leaders*. Additionally, Michael Bernard offered consultation to the CEO on ways to support senior leaders and to reduce some of the ongoing stress associated with the events that were transpiring.

Who participated? Six senior leaders, who were highly talented and positive people, were facing ongoing, unexpected and unfair events largely not of their doing. Their professional reputations were under attack. A major goal, of the crisis intervention, was to re-build resilience.

Why senior leaders need 110%+ of resilience. When people experience unexpected, intense and ongoing highly stressful events (exposure to violence, criticism, rejection, hostility, failure) that they have little control over, two impacts are often observed: 1. They become less able to manage their emotions in all areas of their lives, and 2. They become more vigilant in identifying events as problematic, threatening or challenging. The result can be prolonged and repetitive periods of intense, painful emotional stress and behavioural impairments both at work and home. The good news is that people can learn to minimise the impact of unexpected, tsunami-like events and the emotional wounding experienced, through re-learning and strengthening of their resilience.

The High Performance Mindset at Work – Resilience Program for Leaders. The intensive training conducted over four sessions had the following two foci:

1. Management of negative emotions. A primary tool learnt by the senior leaders, was the use of the ABC model of emotional regulation.
2. Strengthening positivity. The importance of moving attentional focus away from what is not right or negative – to the positive aspects of one's job (and home life).

Outcomes and benefits of HPMW Resilience Training. Within an eight-week period, normal resilience levels of the participants were restored. Levels of job satisfaction returned. Emotional stress significantly decreased. And no longer were participants bringing home unwanted stress and fatigue, which was having a detrimental effect on family life. Participants gained awareness and practice in cognitively restructuring stress-creating beliefs to healthy beliefs. They also (re)-learned self-management, coping skills including: talking to a trusted friend, using relaxation (deep breathing, muscle), recreating – finding something fun to do, exercising, using humour, timing oneself out and using assertive behaviour – including respectfully requesting a change in another's behaviour.

Increasing the Capability and Effectiveness of School Leaders: Impact of the High Performance Mindset at Work Program

1. Internationally the search for answers as to what distinguishes higher performing schools from lower performing schools has led to the consensus that the quality and capacity of school leadership is central.

2. The research on school leadership shows that personal traits, including psychological capability, explain a high proportion of the variation in leadership effectiveness.

3. The goal of this project was to evaluate the impact of a leadership development course developed by Michael Bernard, The High Performance Mindset at Work, on school leaders' capacity and effectiveness. Goals included: a. increased psychological capability by developing the work commitments and resilience that characterise the mindset of top performers as well as overcoming internal work performance blockers; b. greater frequency and effectiveness in use of 'high impact' leadership behaviour identified in research as influencing school organisational effectiveness and students c. reduced stress and increased effectiveness in responding to tough work situations.

4. The Bastow Institute of Educational Leadership advertised an eight-week high HPMW course to school leaders working in Victorian schools.

   28 school leaders participated in the course:
   - 16 principals, 7 assistant principals, 5 expert teachers
   - 5 males, 23 females
   - Years of experience: 1–10 yrs. (1), 11–20 yrs. (11), 21yrs.+ (16)
   - Type of school: secondary (8), primary (16), special (4)

5. The eight-week HPMW course offered at Bastow consisted of:
   - Three-hour face-to-face orientation session attended by all participants, which included completion of pre-course surveys and an introduction to the high performance mindset
   - Six weekly eLearning sessions which participants completed in their own time and space designed to increase their self-awareness and apply elements of a high performance mindset at their work setting
   - Six weekly, group, one-hour webinars, Blackboard Collaborate sessions where participants discussed with each other and engaged in activities that supported application of course material to their work setting
   - Three-hour face-to-face consolidation session attended by all participants, which included completion of post-course surveys and a review of key points and discussion of benefits of the HPMW course.

6. Benefits of the HPMW course included a significant and immediate impact of the HPMW course on participants' capacity and effectiveness. Findings included:
   - ✓ Strengthening of psychological capability including greater self-awareness/self-reflection, positivity, confidence/self-efficacy and calmness in tough work situations
   - ✓ Comments by colleagues of participants reveal changes in leadership behaviour include greater calmness, confidence, positivity, warmth, decisiveness and ability to lead teams
   - ✓ Higher frequency and effectiveness in use of 'high impact' leadership behaviours
   - ✓ Reduction in stress and increase in effectiveness when responding to tough work situations.

89% Effectiveness as a school leader

84% My ability to communicate a clear vision for the school's future

89% Overall confidence to lead

79% My ability to set and communicate goals for improving student learning

95% My ability to provide individual teachers with constructive feedback and an evaluation of their teaching performance

79% My ability to make decisions and communicate how to utilise resources systematically

'I actually feel empowered by my learning and ability to recognise in myself those attributes that need to be modified to improve my leadership... I think.'

Return on investment (ROI)

'Research with engineering managers in a high-tech manufacturing firm has shown that training focused in strengthening psychological resources contributed to a 270% return on investment.' – Journal of Organizational Behavior

If you invest in high performance mindset training, here's what you can expect. Because this form of training needs to be customised for your organisation, you can expect that leadership behaviour you want to see in practice (e.g., performance management discussions) will be more frequent. Additionally, you will see that team leaders and team members not only perform more collaboratively but their individual ability to respond effectively to tough work situations that are crucial to high performance in their roles will be in evidence. The result is better performance, improved results.

LEADERSHIP

Whether you are aspiring to become a leader or want to go from good to great as a leader, your mindset is critical. Here are some thoughts about how to fine tune your mindset for effective leadership.

Neuroleadership

Based on findings from neuro-leadership, we now know that your brain's pre-frontal cortex carries out essential duties for high workplace performance. Consider the question, what is the main influence on leadership behaviour? While organisational culture, incentive schemes and relationships certainly matter, there is now substantial agreement that the main driver of high performance leadership is your inner CEO, which is located in an area of your brain called the pre-frontal cortex. The inner CEO of top executives plays a massive role in integration, planning and regulating leadership behaviour. In high performing leaders, the pre-frontal cortex – which monitors all aspects of how we perform at work – is highly developed and constantly activated.

As you read through the following list which outlines some of the most important duties that your pre-frontal cortex performs ask yourself how well your inner CEO manages each duty, including opportunities for growth. If your inner CEO doesn't function as efficiently as you'd like, fear not – there are a variety of ways to activate your pre-frontal cortex, a few of which I have included.

Sets vision
How clear are your dreams for yourself and your organisation? Your dreams are the magnets that pull you upwards.
Activator: Write down two or three dreams and share them with someone.

Focuses attention

How distracted are you by competing demands, interruptions and internal work performance blockers such as anxiety, anger and procrastination? Do you give sufficient time to the essentials?

Activator: Establish clear boundaries with yourself and others regarding when you need time for yourself, and when you are available to support others.

Monitors work performance

There are four areas of your automatic mindset operating system that require regular vigilance by your 'inner CEO':

1. Work performance (indicators, goals and plans)
2. Performance blockers (external and internal)
3. Skillset (technical, leadership and teamwork)
4. Mindset (self-talk and behaviour).

Activator: Set up a reminder schedule to regularly monitor each area, and work on self-improvement where needed.

Solves problems

When faced with obstacles, how successful are you at applying problem-solving strategies – defining problems, generating alternatives, considering consequences, planning action, and evaluating?

Activator: Apply problem-solving strategies to a problem you are currently faced with by following these steps:

What's the problem?

- What are different ways I can deal with the problem?
- What are the positive and negative short- and long-term consequences of each solution?
- Select the solution with the greatest likelihood of success and least likelihood of negative consequences.
- Formulate a plan and implement the solution.
- Evaluate and, if necessary, revise.

Stimulates creativity

Do you spend the right balance of time harnessing your creativity and engaging in logical thought?

Activator: Be authentic in expressing your ideas without fear of negativity from others. Do not censor yourself when generating novel ideas.

Regulates negative emotions

When you notice that you're experiencing negative emotions – for instance anger, anxiety or sadness – can your inner CEO restore self-management and emotional control though rational thinking and coping skills?

Activator: Try to increase your awareness and notice specific things that trigger your negative emotions. When they arise, take some time to concentrate on your breathing, and when you feel in control, focus your attention back to the situation at hand.

Generates positive emotions

When you're having a bad day or know you have a hard task ahead of you, are you capable of converting negative energy into positive energy?

Activator: Surround yourself with positive and uplifting people.

Maintains a positive self-image

How vulnerable is your self-image to knockbacks, setbacks and lows in work performance?

Activator: Practice positive self-affirmations, for example, 'I appreciate and accept myself no matter what.'

It's sometimes the case that average performing, high potential leaders possess under-developed pre-frontal cortices. By increasing self-awareness and strengthening the way their inner CEO operates, impressive, immediate and sustainable enhancement of work performance occurs.

Let me finish with having you reflect on three questions that are critical for you to answer if you are concerned with talent insufficiency in your senior leadership ranks. These questions are crucial to answer if you need your leaders to do more with less, if too many are under-performing as well as needing them to lead your organisation through big changes.

Are their significant gaps in the work performance mindset of individuals on your leadership team?

What are you doing to make them more aware of and strengthen their high performance mindset?

What would be the benefit to your bottom line of strengthening their work performance mindset?

Changing mindset is the most difficult task of all – and that's what we know most about – our leadership programs are all about strengthening the mindset needed for high performance.

Leadership mindset trumps skillset

If you had $100 to invest in improving your work performance, would you spend it on training skillset or mindset? Which would give the best return on investment?

Research indicates that a high performance mindset is twice as important to high performance outcomes as educational background and technical skills.

A high performance skillset is quite different from a high performance mindset.

Over the past 20 years, researchers investigating leadership have identified a range of skills top leaders possess, and which they engage in effectively and consistently when leading teams and managing others.

High performance skillset

Here's a partial list of the high performance leadership skillset that distinguish exceptional leaders:

- ✓ Communicate a clear vision for the organisation's future
- ✓ Display a high level of energy and enthusiasm to motivate others
- ✓ Encourage staff to share creative and innovative ideas without fear of being criticised or ridiculed
- ✓ Deal with conflict and work to solve problems in a timely fashion
- ✓ Involve members of staff in decision making when it impacts upon their work
- ✓ Model values, including being trustworthy and doing the right thing
- ✓ Focus on what's working well and what's exceptional in individuals, teams and the organisation
- ✓ Identify and build on people's strengths rather than trying to correct their weaknesses, and consider people's strengths when delegating work

✓ Show through actions and words that every employee is valued
✓ Communicate to staff a greater ratio (5:1) of positive feedback than negative feedback.

High performance mindset

Over the same period of time, researchers studying positive psychological capital of highly effective leaders have identified the elements of the work performance mindset of exceptional leaders. Some of these include:
✓ Having a clear vision of what they want to accomplish in the future for themselves and their organisation
✓ Believing that no matter their age, stage or status, they are always developing over time
✓ Having the self-belief in their ability to lead and to be successful
✓ Being optimistic
✓ Believing in the importance of empathy
✓ Possessing a positive, stable self-image and self-acceptance
✓ Being resilient by staying calm in challenging situations
✓ Being authentic; knowing the importance of being true to themselves and what they stand for, and behaving accordingly
✓ Being respectful and valuing others
✓ Making a conscious choice to be aware of the positive rather than negative aspects of a situation, person and what has transpired during the day.

Here's my recommendation on how to invest the $100

If you are a leader in the beginning phases of your career, I'd invest $50 to help become aware of and employ high performance leadership skills. And I'd initially invest $50 into high performance mindset training which will not only increase your work performance, it will multiply the impact of all other leadership and talent management programs you are using. For senior leadership (and I'd include in this recommendation, for your highest performers), I'd invest $90 of the $100 in mindset training and development. Too many high performers fail to take the next step or lose focus and ambition due to issues surrounding…yes, mindset not skillset.

How to bulletproof your employees against work stress

You will know that when stress is extreme for your employees bad things happen – including absenteeism, staff turnover and lowered commitment, work engagement and performance. Additionally, the mental and emotional lives of employees can suffer greatly, particularly under abnormal levels of stress.

As a captain of the ship, you have a duty of care to protect your employees and you can bulletproof them (and yourself) against stress. It takes a bit of preparation and time but it's well worth the effort.

Six causes of work stress

1. Work overload – time/workload pressures;
2. Changing priorities at the last minute;
3. Change in organisational structure and colleagues/reporting;
4. Not being involved in collaborative decision-making that effects your job;
5. Colleagues, including superiors, who engage in unprofessional behaviour, for example, failure to complete assigned tasks at a quality standard; showing disrespect;
6. Performance setbacks – not achieving goals.

How to cure work stress

If you do anything about how often the above stressors occur, that will make a big difference.

There is little question that HR (or you) needs to take a leading role in providing employees with ongoing support to help them cope the mental and emotional strain . This is especially important for new hires – especially during their period of induction and the following months.

Four steps employees can take to reduce stress

1. Supportive relationship. Employees will find it immeasurably helpful to have one or more people at work (and outside) to whom they can go to when highly stressed. An experienced mentor with a high EQ can listen and offer wise counsel.
2. Personal organisation. If time/workload demands are part and parcel of employee's job, it's vital that learning opportunities are provided in the areas of priority setting, time management and delegation.
3. Resilient mindset. The key to much of stress management is the ability to have on hand strategies for coping with different stressors. You need to make these available for employees to learn how not to take things personally and to increase their tolerance combined with coping skills such as self-management, relaxation, mindfulness and assertion (not aggression or passivity).
4. Healthy lifestyle. Stress is partly physiological and when stress-creating hormones like cortisol and high blood pressure are constantly ringing the bell, one's diet, exercise and recreational lives are key buffers. Employees need an opportunity to consider ways to improve their lifestyles and work-life balance.

A boss or HR can discuss and facilitate ways to make support and prioritise these points.

Stress relievers for workers

Work stress management is an investment you can afford to make. It pays off in so many ways.

Mindfulness
Mindfulness is the act of being intensely aware of what you're sensing, thinking and feeling at every moment without interpretation or judgment.

Self-acceptance
Remind yourself that your value and worth as a person should not be determined by what others think of you nor by your achievements or failures at work.

Replay past work achievements
Think back to those times when you felt good about your work and about things that had gone well for you.

Begin your day calmly
Sit for two minutes in the morning and play some relaxation music. Take full deep breaths. Visualise the day ahead going well.

Support
Find some time to talk with someone whom you trust and who knows you, cares about you and who, if possible, appreciates your work achievements.

Time out
Remove yourself from the stressful environment, go for a walk or arrange to work from home.

Do not 'catastrophise'
Keep things in perspective about events at work that are hassles.

Gratitude
Express appreciation to others for what they have done for you as opposed to paying attention to what you need.

SUCCESSFUL SELLING

'The selling process is filled with opportunities for rejection. If that's not enough, frustration and disappointment are also part of the landscape. It's inescapable. There will be prospects who definitely need what you have to sell, but who won't recognise it regardless of what you tell them, show them, or help them experience. There will also be those who recognize the need but refuse to admit that it applies to them or their company. "Others in our industry, but not us," they will say. And, finally, there will be those who recognize and acknowledge the need but will put off taking any action – for reasons no one can explain.'
– David Mattson and Bruce Seidman, authors, *Protect Your Castle*

I am someone who knows full well that the act of selling is filled with frustration, disappointment and daily opportunities for rejection. Over the years, I have met with many prospects in all areas of business to sell them on the importance of mindset and how our learning and development programs achieve what's really hardest to change, people's mindset. My colleagues help decision-makers clearly see that one important element in the behavioural changes (e.g., improved inter-department communication) they want for management and employees could be found in mindset: change mindset, change behaviour.

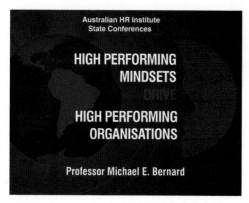

I appeared as an invited keynote speaker at state conferences sponsored by the Australian HR Institute speaking on the need for learning and development, HR programs that focussed on high performance mindset.

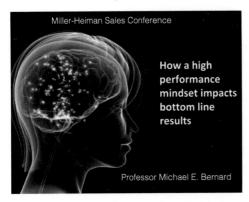

Miller-Heiman Sales Conference

How a high performance mindset impacts bottom line results

Professor Michael E. Bernard

I presented at the annual sales conference of Miller-Heiman Group, an international leader in sales training. Here were my opening remarks:

'Welcome. The overall purpose of today's session is to share with you some of the things we have now learned from research and case studies about the high performance mindset of highly successful salespeople. I'll introduce the latest findings from brain science and the field of positive psychology about what has been discovered about the high performance mindset and how it can be developed. You'll see a number of short movies of people discussing how they have developed a high performance mindset and the amazing impact it has on sales performance.'

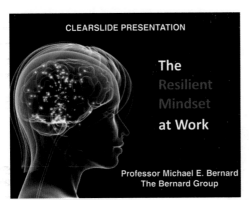

CLEARSLIDE PRESENTATION

The Resilient Mindset at Work

Professor Michael E. Bernard
The Bernard Group

I had the opportunity to present a workshop on resilience in selling to Clearslide, a leader in Sales Enablement and Engagement, along with Gerhard Gschwandtner (Publisher, *Successful Selling*).

The question I continuously pose to my audiences concerned with improving sales performance is this:

What's more important to optimal sales performance skillset or mindset?

And the answer is succinctly expressed by Gerhard: 'The single most important element that will determine your success in sales and in life is your mindset.'

S★LES ST★RS★

A TRAINING PACKAGE TO DEVELOP THE RIGHT ATTITUDES FOR SALES SUCCESS

LEADER'S GUIDE

Along with my colleagues, Eve Ash (Seven Dimensions) and Peter Quarry, we created a training package, Sales Stars, to develop the right attitudes for sales success. Sales Stars has been taken up by numbers of organisations particularly in the retail sector.

The program presents a number of important ideas for dealing with the frequent stresses and strains of selling.

The ABCs of selling

It's really important to know as I have stated throughout this book that your emotions and behaviours are caused by your beliefs and self-talk about what happens to you. The ABC model does a good job of representing these relationships.

What happens in selling is that when you are frequently faced with selling stressors that include losing out on sales, your thinking can shift from a rational, sensible and positive outlook to thinking that is irrational, not sensible and is negative. This is quite normal, but not inevitable.

There are seven types of negative sales beliefs.

1. SELF-BLAMING is when you blame yourself totally because things are not going well.

2. TAKING THINGS PERSONALLY is when you believe you are totally hopeless and useless because you received knockbacks.

3. INACCURATE FORECASTING means that you make negative predictions about your future success.

4. NEEDING IMMEDIATE RESULTS is when you get very stressed when it takes you a long time to make a sale.

5. EXAGGERATING is when bad things happen at work and you blow them out of proportion.

6. APPROVAL SEEKING makes you too concerned about what others think of you and leads to anxiety.

7. COMFORT-SELLING causes you to procrastinate, putting off doing necessary things which are unpleasant and may take a long time.

Disputing

The issue for all of us is whether or not we have – when things get tough – the power to change the way we think about things, in particular, our negative, irrational beliefs. This is no easy feat as negative thinking is very sticky and seems to have a will of its own.

One powerful method to change your self-defeating beliefs is to challenge them using a method called 'disputing'. Disputing requires that you listen to your thinking almost as though you have a third ear. It sometimes is difficult to pick up those aspects of your thinking that are extremely rigid and extreme – these ways of thinking can be hidden away in your subconscious. However, with practice you can become more alert to these destructive ways of thinking. That's when you can use disputing.

Disputing involves you asking yourself three questions about a thought you have discovered you have when you are feeling really crummy about your work.

1. Is what I am thinking sensible?
2. Is what I am thinking true?
3. Is what I am thinking helpful?

When you answer 'yes' to any of these questions, you can then change your thinking to make it more sensible, true and helpful.

Here's an example:

Activating event: Lost third sale in a row.
Beliefs: 'I'm on an endless downward spiral'. (Inaccurate forecasting.)
Consequences: Dejected, weary, reluctant to make any more calls, low confidence.

Dispute:
'Where is the evidence for being on a downward spiral? Isn't sales always about peaks and troughs?'
'Is it sensible and helpful to think this way?'

Change thinking:

'My thinking is shabby.'

'Just because I've lost three sales in a row does not mean I am on a downward spiral. Tomorrow I start afresh!'

How would you expect a change of thinking about three lost sales in a row would effect how the salesperson feels and behaves?

So, it is really, really important to take charge of your self-talk to help protect you and strengthen your RESILIENCE.

Beware catastrophising

Our brains our hard-wired for fight-flight. As part of this attribute, everyone has a tendency when faced with adversity to blow things out of proportion which leads to excess, unnecessary high levels of emotional stress.

'It's awful I didn't meet my monthly targets.'

'It's terrible that a sale I was really close to clinching just fell through.'

'It's horrible that I made a lousy presentation.'

'I can't stand having to visit 10 clients on this hot day.'

When you catch yourself catatastrophising, it's time to change your mindset. Ask yourself using an objective scale of catastrophes, how bad is it really that these things happen to you compared with events that are catastrophic (war, pandemic, natural disaster, serious cancer) and those events that are very bad (divorce, house burns down, redundancy)?

Powerful self-talk that combats my catastrophising: 'This is not as bad as it could be. I can stand things that are bad and that I don't like.'

Protect your self

David Mattson and Bruce Seidman raise an important point concerning self-preservation needed for successful selling:

How will you prevent this 'hostile' environment from having a detrimental impact on your inner core – your psychological well-being? Of course, it is important to take responsibility for your feelings. However, there is more to it than that. No one can enter your castle and harm you or devalue your self-worth. The events of the outer world remain in the outer world.

Human beings of all persuasions in all occupations are extremely and some might say overly sensitive to their own errors, imperfections and failures. As a result, many choose to put themselves down – this is where it is important to maintain a self-accepting and objective view of oneself. 'Yes, I have not been as successful as I want to be and that's too bad, but I know that my self-worth as a person does not come from the outside world – my achievements at work or what others think of me. Now, how am I going to improve my performance?'

So, as much as possible, eliminate negative thinking about yourself. Push yourself through willpower to do everything you have to get done to be successful – no matter what. When you catch yourself stewing rather than doing, go out and do what needs to be done.

HIGH PERFORMANCE MINDSET MENTORING FOR UNIVERSITY STUDENTS

Michael Bernard and Deakin University upper-level Business and Law student mentors

I think universities need to refocus on students. I think this can extend beyond enabling students to think analytically about the knowledge they are being taught and assessed on including the results of their professors' research. I believe the time has come to consider students wholistically, not merely as learning 'objects'. The time is ripe for a paradigm shift for universities (as has occurred in primary/secondary education) to draw and cross the line in the sand between having their mission solely being achievement/research/academics with wellbeing programs being bolted on for the needy to learning, student-centred institutions that have a wider focus.

The Successful Mind
in Study, Work and Life

MENTOR TRAINING PROGRAM

DEAKIN UNIVERSITY
BUSINESS & LAW

Michael E. Bernard, Ph.D.
Professor, University of Melbourne
Melbourne Graduate School of Education

YouCanDoIt!
Education

2020 The Bernard Group

Innovation, innovation, innovation at Deakin University, Faculty of Business and Law

Jen Smith, Manager, Student Experience, was concerned about the rise in mental health issues in students including the stresses and demands of their studies and wanting them to be prepared. She had used our YCDI! Education Mentoring program in the UK with great success a few years ago. She invited me to incorporate in their existing mentoring program of first-year students a program I call The Successful Mind in Study, Work and Life.

I delivered to 150 upper-level, university students the inaugural, first-of-its-kind, online Successful Mind in Study, Work and Life Mentor Training Program. These upper level students mentor 1,500 first-year students annually. These mentors help participating students develop their social-emotional skills research has found contributes to high academic and workplace performance and mental health/ wellbeing at the university level including growth mindset, resilience, mindfulness, optimism, GRIT, self-acceptance, goal setting, time management, character strengths and relationships.

Feedback from mentors on the training was great. Many expressed the view that the SELs taught in our program would benefit them as well as their mentees. And the mentees have moved to weekly online mentoring presentations to their mentees who they report are engaging with the Successful Mind program. The program is also focused on providing university students with high performance attitudes and skills that they can use when focused on their studies. Bravo Deakin for being forward thinking in seeing that university studies should not only cover the academic-technical skills, but also social-emotional domain and holistic preparation of students for their studies and careers.

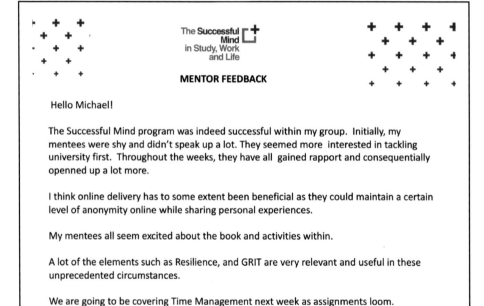

The **Successful Mind**
in Study, Work and Life

MENTOR FEEDBACK

Hello Michael!

The Successful Mind program was indeed successful within my group. Initially, my mentees were shy and didn't speak up a lot. They seemed more interested in tackling university first. Throughout the weeks, they have all gained rapport and consequentially openned up a lot more.

I think online delivery has to some extent been beneficial as they could maintain a certain level of anonymity online while sharing personal experiences.

My mentees all seem excited about the book and activities within.

A lot of the elements such as Resilience, and GRIT are very relevant and useful in these unprecedented circumstances.

We are going to be covering Time Management next week as assignments loom.

I'll keep you posted.

2020 The Bernard Group

While a high performance mindset is indispensable at work, it is equally important as a governing force behind how you operate at home. Have a look.

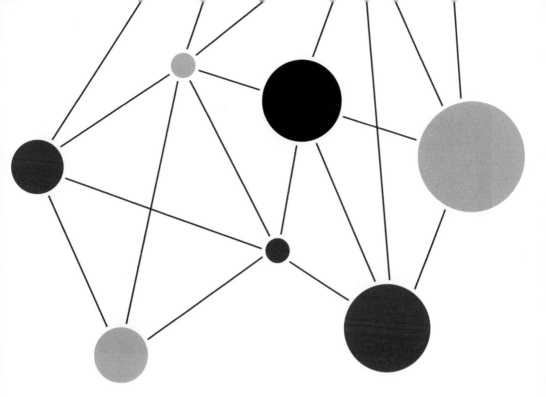

Part 6

Home

'Home means an enjoyable, happy place where you can live, laugh and learn. It's somewhere where you are loved, respected, and cared for. When you look at it from the outside,
home is just a house. A building.'
- meaningofhome.ca

'Family might be defined as a group of people who are related to each other, but it's more than that. It's a meaningful connection, an experience. It's an incredible and unbreakable bond – created by mothers, fathers, sisters, brothers. It's comfort in a world of uncertainty. It's a shoulder to lean on. It's a source of inspiration. It's love and support. It's that warm and fuzzy feeling.
It's wonderful, and it's necessary.'
- Lydia Sweatt, Web Producer, SUCCESS.com

'A family that supports one another thrives.'
- Gabrielle Applebury, marriage and family therapist

'A happy family is but an earlier heaven.'
- George Bernard Shaw, playwright

STRONG RELATIONSHIPS

My home is my most important place. That's because of the relationships I enjoy with my two children and wife. I have always worked from home as much as possible to be close to my family. I have been a very passionate parent – staying connected and always wanting to do the very best for my kids. And I've done my best to be a loving, caring and respectful partner to my wife, Patricia. Through the efforts of each of my family members, we have remained a very close family.

How much does mindset and the mindset of family members effect the quality of relationships at home? What aspects of a high performance matter in terms of building strong relationships, solving relationship problems, being happy and fulfilled at home, the parenting strengths we need to raise positive children and in encouraging a high performance mindset in our kids? That's what this part of the book is about.

There are several aspects of a high performing mindset that help develop positive relationships at home.

Commitment to Others

As discussed in Part 2 of this book, a Commitment to Others means that you have a strong desire and dedication to support and help all members of your family of all ages to grow, learn and advance without expecting anything back in return.

With a strong Commitment to Others as part of your moral compass, you communicate to all members of your family a positive, optimistic outlook for their future and you display the resilience needed by everyone to overcome the tough situations that occur in all families and to each family member when they venture out in the world.

The beliefs that define this commitment that you want to action as often as possible are accepting others unconditionally, showing empathy by trying to understand what others are feeling and how they see the lay of the land, valuing respect by treating everyone with consideration and regard even when you disagree with their opinions or don't like their behaviour, being there when someone needs support and help and providing where necessary lots of constructive positive feedback when people do the wrong thing.

Here are actions that demonstrate you have a high strong Commitment to Others.

1. Helping others grow and develop to be the best they can be and overcoming their problems.
2. Giving, including volunteering, and not expecting anything back in return.
3. Respecting people who are different.
4. Making people feel valued including the tasks they perform.
5. Empathy towards people experiencing difficulties.
6. Respect for the differences of opinion and behaviour.
7. Not judging people by their behaviour.
8. Seeing retaliation for perceived injustice or unfairness as unnecessary and, oftentimes, counter-productive.

PATRICIA BERNARD, COMMITMENT TO FAMILY

Having grown up in an Italian family and culture, my father and mother provided constant, unconditional love, support and caring every day. A very strong commitment to family was modelled and reinforced in me from the time I can remember. I could not help but adopt this same commitment with my own family and to my extended family and friends.

There are many times that this commitment gets tested and working tirelessly to provide for your loved ones can create fractures where your resolve manages to get you through, especially during tough times when you find yourself selfishly and sometimes rightly so wondering 'When will I get "me" time again? When can I commit to just myself?' When my resolve is tested to give when and where needed, I have always found the effort that goes along with a strong commitment to my own family helps me persevere.

With my husband, Michael, the author of this book, raising two fine human beings, now in their adult years, was the greatest commitment of my life. My new family life was stretched in exciting but at times challenging ways from the day our children were born.

With Michael's enormous dedication to his lifelong work and moving home several times to support him, our family time was often compromised. But one thing we both were dedicated to was our commitment and love for our family. With the two sides of our extended family across three continents, we spent years of family time maintaining as close contact as we could which meant flying around the world throughout our children's childhood to just visit family. Taking our jobs and sometimes our home along the way meant we had to juggle multiple scenarios and sacrifice time, effort and money to maintain a closeness to family. Both Michael and I were committed to our families and we felt we wanted to make sure that our children did not miss out on the opportunity to know their grandparents and extended family members while growing up.

In addition to keeping our family closely connected, we also wanted to be as involved in our kid's schooling and the community as much as possible. This allowed us to be involved when needed, be aware of their efforts and experiences and as much as possible provide them the one thing children yearn for, "parent's attention" without going over the top.

I decided there wasn't enough room in our family for two career-focused parents. I chose to be a 'stay at home parent' so I could be the support Michael and the children needed. Having our own business to help develop and grow also provided me this opportunity.

Life plays full circle and many years later I now find I'm not mothering my children anymore but my own dear mother as she spends her twilight years in aged care affected by multiple conditions that provide her with no independence. Fortunately, she is still able to recognise those closest to her and at the time of writing this I find myself, with the support of a loving family, able to commit to her needs so that she is cared for in the best way possible. In doing so, I've learned to be patient, to not expect anything in return, to accept that times are tough, to go without 'me time' because there isn't time left at the end of the day and to put other's needs first without being a martyr, to recognise when someone is needy and try and support them. In recent years my commitment to the elderly (not just my mother) has been a rewarding one. Offering compassion and duty of care to those who were committed to giving us a good life as possible seems a fair and loving way to farewell them.

Resilience

To my way of thinking, your resilience is totally necessary for your family, partner and kids to be successful and happy.

Homelife has its ups and downs – and you will have experienced multiple tough situations that have the potential to send you and family into a downward spiral. You may have completed the *Inventory of Tough Situations at Home* in Part 4 so you will know what I am talking about.

CASE STUDY. A SON WHO TEACHES HIS DAD ABOUT RESILIENCE – 'YOU GOTTA THINK'

One day when my son Jonathon, grade 4, was getting ready to leave for school, I asked to have a look at his previous night's homework (which I often did to make sure he was on the right track and didn't need help). Jonathon sheepishly fished out from his school bag an English writing assignment due that day. As I looked over his work, I could feel the temperature of my emotions skyrocketing – he had written several paragraphs in pencil with handwriting that I could hardly decipher. Without thinking, I yelled, 'What the hell is this? This is disgraceful! Are you trying to embarrass me in front of your teacher when you hand this in? You can't go to school until you re-do this assignment. Do it now!' (In my defence, you should know that I have never spanked either of my kids and rarely yelled at them. Promise.) Jonathon burst out crying and ran upstairs to his room. I remember thinking to myself, 'Well done Dad, you handled that really well. Jonathon was in the wrong. He should have taken greater care with his homework. I shouldn't have yelled. But I won't be emotionally blackmailed by his tears' – and by this time I was sprinting up the stairs to apologise. There was Jonathon, sitting on his bed still crying, starting to re-write his assignment. 'Jonathon, you did the wrong thing by rushing and not checking over your assignment. But I shouldn't have yelled. I apologise.' Jonathon looked up at me and wiping his tears from his eyes said… 'That's OK Dad, you just didn't think.'

I had started the day as I always did – with a positive outlook and demeanour, wanting to do the best for everyone at home. Then a tough situation took me by surprise. I experienced loads of anger, worry and I felt down – all at the same time. My positive performance as a parent quickly descended into negativity. Fortunately, I bottomed out very quickly, took control of how upset I was and rebounded to the situation to solve a problem – and to go one better. I learnt that sometimes I just don't think about the best way to handle a tough situation, I just react. That's the interesting thing about resilience. No matter how developed it is, it can desert you when you need it the most – when your emotions run very strong.

10 THINGS TO DO TO BE RESILIENT

1. Be aware of how upset you are (use the Emotional Thermometer).
2. Consider the negative consequences of losing control of your emotions and allowing them to rule your behaviour – for the worse.
3. It is OK to be upset (don't beat yourself up). But also remind yourself of the power you have to manage your emotions and that being medium rather than extremely upset is an option and means you are still in control and capable of making good decisions.
4. Do not blow the badness of the event out of proportion.
5. While you may not like a family member's behaviour, you can definitely tolerate it.
6. No matter their age, everyone is still learning how best to get along – everyone makes mistakes and everybody has issues that can lead to negative behaviour.
7. Take a few slow, deep breaths to relax.
8. If you have to, remove yourself from the situation until you are calmer.
9. Discuss the problem with a sympathetic listener.
10. Distract yourself by listening to music, taking a bath, or going for a walk.

Strong relationships with your kids as well as with your partner and parents require that you have a strong ability to manage your emotions. You have to because others may not be so good at managing their emotions – and what they say and do when their emotions are extreme can damage relationships – at least temporarily. You are needed to steady everyone's ship through rocky water.

Emotional management

My friend Ray DiGiuseppe said years ago that Sigmund Freud got it wrong when he wrote that our strongest emotions are directed towards our parents. Ray said that we have the strongest emotions about our kids and I reckon he was 1000% correct.

The desire for self-management of emotions needs to be hard-wired into your brain – a part of your commitment to having a fantastic family. I say desire because as you have seen in the way I responded to Jonathon, desire for doing the right things can be sabotaged by strong emotional impulses.

Here's what I have learnt about self-management of emotions or what can be called *emotional problem solving*. (You can also review what I wrote about the ABCs in Part 4. Resilience.)

I start off with a fundamental understanding of where my emotions come from.

I do not blame my partner or kids or my world for what I feel when I am faced with a tough situation, even when someone is being self-centred, selfish or just plain mean. At these times, I still know that I make myself angry – as well as anxious or depressed.

THINGS ARE NEITHER GOOD NOR BAD BUT THINKING MAKES IT SO

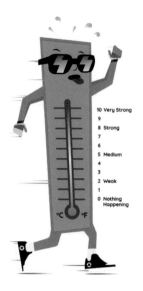

I remind myself that I have choices in how upset I get depending on my outlook and that when I get extremely or overly angry, worried or down about something going on at home, I don't think clearly about the best way to respond and I can rush to solve the problem. And I can be in a whole lot of pain.

The ABC model of emotional problem solving has taught me a great lesson about how to calm myself down or stay calm. This is a great power to have.

A = activating event, adversity (a tough situation)
B = beliefs (the way you think about the A)
C = consequences (how you feel and behave)

When I find myself extremely upset about a tough situation, I identify as best I can my extreme, rigid thoughts about the situation, thoughts that are not sensible, not true and not helpful. Then I try to re-think the situation using more flexible, moderate self-talk that is sensible, true and helpful.

Here are examples of different types of thinking that lead to strong emotions and how to change your thinking using the ABC model.

1. Am I blowing the badness of the event out of proportion? Am I catastrophising? If 'yes,' I change my thinking to: 'This is bad, but not the worst thing that could happen.'
2. Am I thinking that I must always be the perfect partner or parent and never make mistakes? If 'yes,' I change my thinking to: 'While I strongly prefer to do my very best at home, it doesn't make sense to think I must always be successful because like everyone else, I am fallible.'
3. Am I thinking I need the approval of others for how well I behave towards my family? If 'yes,' I change my thinking to 'Just because I like to be approved of and thought highly of by others, I don't need approval to survive - I only need food, water and shelter.'

4. Am I thinking that when one of my family behaves inconsiderately, disrespectfully or unfairly, that he or she is a total loser or a total creep? If 'yes,' I change my thinking to: 'I prefer my partner/son/daughter to behave fairly, generously of spirit and in the way I behave towards them, but when he or she doesn't, that's tough. It doesn't say anything about his or her overall value or worthiness. Don't condemn the sinner for the sin.'
5. Am I thinking that I cannot stand nor tolerate my family member's behaviour? If 'yes,' I change my thinking to, 'I can bloody well cope with this behaviour, I have for all these years and it hasn't killed me yet. I can stand things I don't like.'

The alternative ways of thinking when well-practiced and often always help me to stay calmer.

RELATIONSHIP PROBLEMS

Here's a useful way to think about relationship problems you can have at home. If it appeals, wire it into the way you think about a family member whose behaviour you are finding doesn't live up to expectations.

Relationship dissatisfaction occurs when your partner (or other family member) does not provide what you want or provides what you don't want. Relationship dissatisfaction is not an uncommon condition in long-standing relationships and often results from changes in one or both of you over the years. Dissatisfaction does not mean there is anything wrong with your relationship or your partner.

CASE STUDY. WENDY AND JIM HOWARD, MARRIED 18 YEARS

Early in her relationship with her husband, Wendy Howard was quite happy to give up her job in order to take care of her two children on a full-time basis and was also willing to shoulder most of the domestic responsibilities of cooking, cleaning and shopping. As the years went by and her children grew older, Wendy began to want more time for herself during the week, so that she could set up a business of her own at home which involved her designing creative displays for department and other retail stores. When she made her wishes known to her husband Jim and enlisted his cooperation in sharing domestic responsibilities, Jim seemed willing enough, but never actually managed to do much of the work.

In this scenario, both Wendy and Jim would likely experience a reduction in the satisfaction with their relationship. Both parties would experience a range of normal, healthy negative emotions such as annoyance, irritation or concern. The dissatisfaction in the Howard relationship may be short-lived until a solution is found; however, if no solution is found, if the dissatisfaction lasts too long, it may threaten the long-term survival of the relationship.

On the other hand, a *relationship disturbance* occurs when you or your partner become extremely upset (anxious, enraged, depressed) about a problem in the relationship and engage in extremely negative behaviour towards the other person that generally leads to an escalation of your difficulties. In the case of the Howards, if Jim became extremely upset because of Wendy's desire for more independence and for him to do more of the housework, or if Wendy because of Jim's reluctance to share in home duties became furious with him, then their emotional reactions towards each other represents a relationship disturbance.

When either or both partners become overly upset about a problem that exists in the relationship, then it is better that the relationship disturbance be resolved (emotion calmed down) before the issue which is causing the relationship dissatisfaction can be solved.

Said in a simple way, when you or someone else at home (partner, kids, grandparents) become overly upset about some aspect of each other's behaviour, it is best for each party to calm themselves down, first making themselves feel annoyed or sorry but not enraged in order to be able to solve the problem.

In summary, (1) understand that extreme emotional reactions to problems between family members are generally harmful to the relationship, (2) accept the idea that the way one or both members of the relationship can through their thinking create extreme emotions like rage or depression or excessive anxiety that converts the relationship dissatisfaction to a relationship disturbance, (3) by choosing to re-think the situation using more flexible, moderate self-talk that is sensible, true and helpful, calmer heads will prevail and (4) Don't stand in judgment of people based on their behaviour. Give people the right to be wrong and then figure out ways to try to get them to change their behaviour.

I often call on The Serenity Prayer to help me deal with issues in my family: Grant me the courage to change those things that I can, the serenity to accept those things that I cannot, and the wisdom to know the difference.

HAPPINESS AT HOME

Managing stress, especially if you are a parent, and helping everyone at home to flourish leads to happy and fulfilled families.

Flourishing

Family life should not just be about survival and peaceful co-existence. One important aspect of mindset is helping everyone to flourish.

Flourishing Families
(https://magazine.byu.edu/article/families-that-flourish/)

Researchers have found the following are powerful factors in making family life and marriages stronger, happier, and more stable.

- **Freely forgive.** Let go of hurts quickly and check in with your spouse and children about whether they see you as forgiving.
- **Be kind.** Be patient, speak kindly, and assume good motives in other family members.
- **Be committed.** Speak and act in ways that show your family you're in it for the long haul.

- **Be willing to sacrifice.** Understand that your way isn't always the best way, and you might have to give up things you want or need for the greater good of your family.
- **Don't be relationally aggressive.** Don't talk badly about each other to other people, don't use the silent treatment, and don't dismiss another family member's feelings.

In his book, *Flourish,* psychologist Martin Seligman, the founder of Positive Psychology, set out an approach for helping people to flourish in life and find the happiness we all desire. Flourishing is the word Martin Seligman uses to describe the highest level or gold standard of happiness and well-being.

Seligman named his approach to a flourishing life as PERMA an acronym that identifies the five essential elements required for us to attain a fulfilling and happy life. The more often you experience these elements, the greater your level of life satisfaction, happiness and flourishing. The five PERMA elements are: P = Positive Emotions E = Engagement R = Positive Relationships M = Meaning A = Achievement/Accomplishment.

Anything can sound good in theory, but putting the five PERMA, elements into place in our lives doesn't have to be complicated or difficult if we are committed to making the most of ourselves. Often theory is not as far removed from reality as we think, and being positive and engaged, and finding meaning in our relationships and achievements is pretty much what most of us ideally want our lives, including our parenting, to reflect.

Positive emotions. There's little that beats having a positive emotion. Ask any long distance runner and they'll tell you how good it feels when the endorphins kick in. The good news is we don't have to be a long distance runner to experience feelings of well-being. Positive emotions can also induce a natural high. Gratitude, pleasure, fulfilment, peace, satisfaction and inspiration are some of the positive emotions we can savour and celebrate. By practising mindfulness (living in the moment) we can celebrate our families by making the most of our kids' milestones and memorable occasions. Keep a journal to discover those events that occur during the day that lead you to experience different positive emotions. Build these events in your life on as regular a basis as possible.

Engagement. Engaging with all members of our family is foundational to bonding and building strong relationships. Most of us know how disconnected we can feel when we're trying to accomplish one task and the mobile rings, or we're still in work mode thinking of tomorrow's strategy meeting, or we have to drop everything to put out someone else's spot fire. Only when we're fully engaged in concentrating on the task at hand, free of distractions, can we hope to experience the pleasure of being 'lost' to the world. Little kids are good at this – they can play or create, oblivious to what's happening around them. As adults however, we may need to rediscover this skill, so that when we connect with our family we are helping to form a secure base for their growth and development. Bottom line here is that it is a good investment towards flourishing to spend quality time with your family away from your physical and mental distractions.

Relationships. A relationship that isn't positive is probably not worth having. As humans, some of the reasons we strive to work at meaningful relationships are to be happier, more secure, feel cared for and enjoy the spin-offs such as empathy, friendship, strength and support. Relationships are core to our feelings of well-being and taking the time and effort to build a strong relationship with our child as well as our partner, extended family, friends and neighbours will give us pleasure as well. Some people can become so engrossed in work commitments or in raising a family they fail to put in the time necessary to stay connected and to reap the rewards. Also, it is far too easy to subtly disengage from our partners, devoting our energy and time to our children. Keep in mind that personal relationships are hugely important to our happiness as a parent and fulfilment as a person. Whether it is reaching out to family or friends in an hour of need or simply scheduling a few hours to be with a friend. These are likely to be behaviours within your reach, so stretch yourself towards others.

Meaning. Research suggests that the existence of children in our lives does not increase levels of happiness. However, when having children fills a greater purpose of believing in and serving someone and something greater than ourselves, our happiness and satisfaction in raising children increases enormously. In choosing to have kids, the research suggests the decision to bring a child into the world can be based on meaning. As parents, maintaining high levels of meaning occurs when we focus on the bigger picture of giving ourselves unconditionally to another person. We can also make conscious efforts at keeping in mind the important place that our children have within our broader and intergenerational family. So, reflect on the meaning of parenting and not just the everyday tasks.

Achievement and Accomplishment. Helping to build a happy home is a significant achievement. Along the way, there are numerous small achievements – some of them child-centred, some parent-centred and some partner-centred. We can experience child-centred feelings of achievement when children first manage to sleep through the night, or when they're fully toilet trained, or when they can at long last read a book for themselves. Parent-centred accomplishments can often be a little more difficult to achieve. These require us to put time and effort into achieving goals outside those of parenting, and it is important that 'me' time is kept separate from parental responsibilities. Partner-centred feelings of accomplishment occur when we show our empathy, acceptance and understanding when our partner is having a bad day. Feeling good about our personal achievements and ourselves helps to support our positive mindset as parents. Developing and nurturing the PERMA principles helps us to maintain feelings of well-being and get the most from life. PERMA principles also help us as parents to enjoy our kids, not just raise them.

We designed the Flourishing Menu (accompanying page) as something you could share with your family to get the flourishing ball rolling for all members of your household.

Flourishing Menu

Daily actions parents and children can take

SEASONING TIP:

The healthiest diet is when parents and children put these actions into practice as often as they can.

The dishes on this menu are the very best actions for parents and children to take that lead to happy and productive lives. We suggest you start by serving up one or two to the whole family and see who likes what. They are delicious. And best of all, the dishes are FREE!

1st Course		
Health	Healthy Living	Be active, exercise, play, eat well, relax
	Acceptance	Be comfortable with who you are, don't take things personally
	Pursuing Interests	Discover and spend time in absorbing activities that interest you
	Hope	Start today believing that good things can happen
	Positive Thinking	Focus on what is good, inside and out
	Resilience	Stay calm, bounce back
	Be Grateful	Notice the good things people do and say 'thanks'

2nd Course		
Relationships	Connect	Talk and meet with people at work, home and in your community
	Give	Do nice things for others
	Belong	Join a group, team or organisation
	Respect	Say things that show you value people and what they do
	Citizenship	Do things to make your community a safer and better place

3rd Course		
Accomplishment	Growth	Know that you develop as a person through life experience and continuous learning
	Set Goals	Decide what you need to get done and get on with it
	Be Confident	Think, 'I can do it' and act like you mean it
	Persist	Give things that extra effort until they are complete
	Teamwork	Find ways to work with others to get things done

When these dishes are served to your family, you'll see everyone flourish. Serve them as often as possible.

Managing Stress

When it comes to stress, there's an undeniable fact: we all need some level of stress to function as a human being. However, when that level of stress becomes 'distress' then we need to learn new ways to cope and manage our emotions and our workload.

The secret to stress management at home is to understand what makes us feel stressed (stressors), learn to recognise the symptoms of stress, and then find strategies and/or develop ways to adjust our responses to stress to keep it at a manageable level.

Of all the jobs we undertake, parenting in particular is about learning on the job. That means it's going to be a very steep learning curve at times.

There are plenty of guidebooks to consult, but who's got time to sit down and read three chapters on getting baby to sleep while the crying continues or go online to discover how to stop bad behaviour when the kids have lost it totally? Expect stress at times – it's all part of the job description.

How to recognise symptoms of stress. The stress response is our body's way of protecting us. Stress helps us stay alert, meet challenges, focus on what we're doing, tap into our source of energy, and in instances of 'fight or flight' galvanise us into action to avoid danger. However, the reality is that stress has a way of creeping up on us unawares. It's easy to get used to levels of stress and ignore the fact that they're beginning to take a toll on our mind, our body and ultimately, our behaviour.

In recognising stress, we need to stop and take on board whether we're exhibiting any common signs.

These can include:

- Mood swings, distraction
- Inability to concentrate or make decisions
- Unable to relax or consistently feeling agitated, anxious, worried or overwhelmed
- Problems with memory
- Short temper, frustration, aggression
- Physical symptoms such as aches, pains, rashes, nausea, dizziness, recurring colds or flu
- Pessimistic outlook on life, constantly feeling down, depression
- Not sleeping properly, tiredness
- Relationship or employment problems.

Stress is often exacerbated not only by our failure to recognise signs, but also by our response to stressors through faulty beliefs, thoughts and actions following certain situations and events. We can fall into the trap of thinking a situation or event is stressful, because we believe it to be so. This may not necessarily be the case, and often it pays to sit down and re-think or talk through perceived causes of stress with a partner, family or friend, to get a more balanced perspective.

Parenting and stress. Parenting can be stressful – even with the best behaved kids on the block. Kids are kids – they will act out their frustrations, misbehave, and defy authority. They will cause us pain of some sort, sometime, somehow. And as for the planets being aligned as regards our employment, housing, family, health and levels of happiness, unfortunately the world has a way of occasionally shifting on its axis to give our foundations a severe shake. Stress happens.

Parenting is one area where it's easy to feel out of control. Being a carer, role model, teacher and nurturer means we are constantly tapping into our physical and emotional reserves and/or limited life experience in raising children.

Choosing to take responsibility for our own emotions is important. When the parenting journey gets tough, a positive outlook, rational self-talk, a balanced perspective and a sense of humour will help to get us through. Our kids are not responsible for our anxieties and emotional tension. Children will undoubtedly make mistakes, as will parents. It's all perfectly natural, and all part of being a parent.

When it comes to parenting, it pays to have a realistic attitude. What is unrealistic about the job of parenting is to have unrealistic and unattainable high ideals and expectations. The perfect child, home, school, relationship or lifestyle does not exist. Every child is unique, as will be their upbringing. Making comparisons or trying to live up to another family's successes or achievements can so often create stress and feelings of frustration for us.

With each developmental stage of childhood, new stressors are bound to emerge. Most often, a decision needs to be made on the spot, without the luxury of time to think things through or talk it over with family or friends. Being prepared for certain aspects of parenting, such as agreed strategies on discipline or behaviour for example, helps to not only provide consistency for the child, but also keep our stress levels manageable for the times when our buttons are being pushed.

Team parent. Parenting is teamwork. If you have a partner, try laying some ground rules together. These can include your preferences for parenting styles, what you both want and expect from parenting, strategies for partnering and coping and what support networks you can tap into if needed. If you are a single parent, maybe think about seeking out significant adults within family or friends, who can support both you and your style of parenting. Where possible, as a family unit, work on nurturing and developing relationships that are mutually supportive, empathetic, and encouraging. Knowing you have back up can be hugely significant in stress management. From an early age, children can be encouraged to know that as part of your family they can help around the house. Daily chores and tasks (however small) help them to learn about responsibility, ownership, and cooperation. Regardless of whether you decide on in-house care for your children or you opt for day-care outside the home, let your carers know your preferences for parenting. This way, carers can be aligned with your philosophy and be partners in supporting your strategies.

Parents are people too. Raising young children can be everything from exhilarating to exhausting. Just because our child is asleep, it doesn't necessarily mean that this time is our own or that their downtime means we have hours to ourselves to pursue an interest. The responsibility of caring for small children is constant and it can be easy to focus on our child's development and interests and forget that as parents we are people too. Making time for ourselves isn't so much selfish as essential. It can be difficult to juggle full-time work, a social life and interests outside family, but adult time away from children can often provide much needed balance, perspective and stimulation. 'Me' time means we have an opportunity to relax, catch a movie, coffee with friends, or enjoy a special hobby. 'Me' time also means that we can return to the job of parenting refreshed and ready for special time with our kids. Regardless of whether you are parenting with a partner or going solo, however small the window of opportunity, make some time for yourself on a regular basis. A coffee with other young mums or dads is also a great way to talk through problems, compare notes and enjoy some adult company. If you have a trusted babysitter, make the most of a night out or an afternoon shopping or a stroll in the park in the sun.

10 STEPS TO STRESS REDUCTION

1. The mind/body makeover. Eat well, exercise, catch up on sleep or watch caffeine levels. Try getting up half an hour earlier in the morning just to have some special time to yourself before the rest of the family starts their day.

2. Non-technology time. If technology is ruling your life, experiment with down times for emails, texts, tweets and time and energy spent on social media websites.

3. Learn to say no. Favours for family and friends, projects around the house, social activities, invitations, additional work commitments – learn to say no to the things you can't achieve rather than run yourself ragged trying.

4. Rethink priorities. Not everything is urgent, not everything is a 'must' or a 'should'. List those things that have to be done, and practise making the distinction between needs and preferences.

5. Keep communication lines open. Talk to your partner, your kids, family, friends, day-care and preschool staff. Try to keep up with what's going on, what's coming up and be one step ahead of where problems might be emerging

6. Don't rely on memory. Missing an appointment, forgetting lunch with friends or being late for pickup can create instant stress. If it has to be remembered, remind yourself – using lists, Outlook, a diary, smartphone or tablet.

7. Relax standards. Domestics are always happy to wait until someone steps in, and the world has a tendency to keep spinning even if we haven't had time to bake, wash cars, water the pot plants or sew on a button.

8. Be mindful. Mindfulness is all about living in the moment, making the most of right now, enjoying what life has in store for us today. Continually projecting forward or back to what has to be done or what should have been done can rob us of the enjoyment of what we're currently doing.

9. Organisation. Keep a spare set of keys, make sure the contact list for day-care, family, doctor, preschool etc. is up to date, allow that extra ten or fifteen minutes to get to an appointment on time, try to keep a lid on organisation at home and the workplace.

10. Breathe in, breathe out. When stressed, try stretching or stopping to take some deep breaths or sit for ten minutes with your eyes closed and let your body just relax. If you have time, try writing thoughts in a journal, plugging calming music into the iPod, or practise meditation or yoga... any preferred activity that helps you to feel less overwhelmed.

PARENTING STRENGTHS

In order to make your commitment to being a successful parent a reality, it will be important for you to know about different parenting practices that research indicates contribute to positive outcomes for your children.

There is lots of advice and warnings about what not to do as a parent if you want your children to turn out all right. 'Don't be too strict.' 'Do not be too lax.' 'Don't protect your child from frustration.' 'The more responsibility you take for your children's behaviour, the less responsibility they take for themselves.' 'Do not let your emotions get out of control.' 'Do not expect too much of your child, make your expectations realistic.'

It can get a bit depressing to hear about all the negative statistics and problems this generation is experiencing and how little influence parents have over our children especially as they grow older in comparison to the influence of their peers and the media.

There is room for optimism. Research continues to show that parents exert a very powerful influence over their children's habits and behaviours whether they know it or not, especially when their children never appear to be listening!

Research indicates that parents who are kind but firm in their style of parenting have kids that turn out to be good kids and successful in what they do.

Kind and firm child rearing practice is the preferred and skilled form of parenting. Parents who raise their children in this fashion talk and reason with them about objectionable behaviour, focus on the behaviour but do not blame the child, set limits with clear consequences for rule violations, set punishment that is related to rule learning, not blame, sometimes frustrate their child when necessary, apply reasonable pressure to teach self-discipline and delay of gratification, never punish out of anger and frequently praise and show love.

We also know that emotionally happy children have parents who teach them self-acceptance. Here's what Albert Ellis, founder of one of the world's most powerful forms of counselling and therapy, Rational Emotive Behaviour Therapy, has written about how parents can communicate self-acceptance to their children:

> Teach children to never rate themselves in terms of their behaviour and to separate judgments of their actions from judgments of self-worth. Encourage them to acknowledge and accept responsibility for their traits and behaviours – both good and bad without evaluating themselves as good or bad. Help combat children's tendencies towards self-downing by reminding them they are made up of many good qualities (and some that are not so helpful) and that they do not lose their good qualities when bad things happen. Explain to children that all human beings are capable and likeable in their unique ways and, therefore, it is good for children to accept themselves unconditionally without having to prove themselves.

The current parenting research reveals that in order to exert a positive influence over children, parents need to have many different parenting skills or strengths that they call on when interacting with their children on a daily basis.

Here are some of the most important parenting strengths that constitute a high performance mindset for raising children.

Develop a positive parent-child relationship

- Spend extra 'special time' with your child.
- Give your child plenty of affection.
- Actively listen to your child without interrupting.
- Refrain from using a negative tone of voice.
- Be emotionally resilient and calm when faced with your child's imperfections.

Communicate high, realistic expectations for your child's achievement and behaviour

- Communicate from time to time that you expect your child to do the best s/he can in school.
- Discuss expectations or rules for behaviour (e.g., speaking respectfully, homework curfew, drinking and the consequences for breaking rules).
- Recognise your child when s/he has worked hard and made good behavioural choices.
- Consistently enforce consequences (do what you say you are going to do).
- Examine homework and have your child redo work that is sloppy and reveals little application.

Provide your child with special responsibilities and involvement in decision-making

- Allow your child to 'have a say' when it comes to making decisions about the ways things are done at home, including setting home rules.

- Offer your child opportunities to be in charge of something important (age-appropriate, e.g. taking care of a family pet).
- Provide your child with choices as to when s/he is going to do something (e.g., homework before or after dinner).
- Include your child in planning special family events and activities.

Support your child's interests

- Encourage your child to pursue his/ her own interests, rather than your interests.
- Find out what interests your child and provide experiences of these interests (e.g., if you have an artistic child, locate extra-curricular art classes and activities, or if you have a child with technical-mechanical activities, locate extra-curricular activities that accommodate these interests e.g., woodworking class).

Be interested and involved in your child's education

- Show interest in what your child is learning in different classes/subjects at school (e.g., ask questions).
- Get to know who your child's teachers are, and their names.
- Be available to help your child when s/he has a problem with schoolwork.
- Attend school events offered to parents (e.g., parent-teacher association, Coffee Break).
- Join a school committee.

Motivate your child's learning

- For homework your child finds difficult or boring/uninteresting, provide lots of praise when work is being accomplished.
- For homework your child finds interesting and pleasurable, avoid providing too much praise; instead, encourage your child's further learning and interest in the subject.
- Communicate your belief that with effort, your child can be successful in school.

Emotionally coach your children

- When your children are upset, be aware of their emotions. Stay calm paying attention to their feelings so you can respond sensitively.
- When your children are upset, recognise this time as an opportunity to be close to them and to teach them about emotions.
- Listen to your children with a great deal of empathy without interrupting with advice.
- Communicate that you understand what they are feeling.
- Help your children find the words to describe how they are feeling inside.
- When you observe your children being emotional, first set limits for what is and what is not acceptable behaviour. Then discuss ways to stay calm as well as different things they can do solve the problem they are faced with.

Be a positive person for your children

- Control your own negative emotions and stress through exercise, diet, recreation, relaxation and positive thinking so that they do not effect your children badly. Focus on what is going right in your life so you experience fun, excitement and pleasure.
- Plan for moments with your children when you are 100 per cent involved with what they are doing and are not distracted by outside events (e.g., cell phone).
- Your partner and yourself should try to maintain high levels of energy and resolve conflicts with each other in calm and constructive ways including not blaming each other and expressing gratitude and affection.
- Be aware of what it means to be a parent and try to instil in your family over time through things you do together an appreciation of the importance of good connections among family members.
- Set goals for what you want to accomplish both as a person and as a parent. Set about charting a course of action and overcoming obstacles that help you to accomplish goals.

Is it ever too late to incorporate these strengths into your high performance parenting mindset? Fortunately, parenting does not come with a use-by-date. All parents learn from their experiences and as a result have great potential for how they go about their parenting. Having well developed parenting strengths does not guarantee lifelong happiness and success for children. Sometimes, events beyond our control impact our children in harmful ways. However, the more we use strengths – and the more we learn from discussions with others and from reading books and articles – the more likely the case that our children will be set on their way with sufficient positivity and momentum for them to develop their unique potential to live fulfilled and rewarding lives.

HIGH PERFORMANCE MINDSET FOR YOUR KIDS

Knowing the importance of mindset in everything that we do, one of the more important things you can focus on in raising and guiding your children is to provide them with positive attitudes and social-emotional skills which together combine into a high performance mindset. You can see from our poster the 12 positive attitudes that are the foundation on which your children's lives sits. These positive attitudes form the basis for strong commitments to success, others and self. These 12 attitudes nourish and support the five social-emotional skills you can see above the house's roof that help power your children to overcome adversity and continue to strive for success and happiness.

Positive Attitudes

Here are the 12 positive attitudes to explain, model and reinforce in children.

Accepting Myself – I am proud of my positive strengths and differences without ignoring my negative characteristics. I accept myself without rating my overall value and self-worth poorly when negative events occur.

Taking Risks – I want to be successful, but I don't have to be. It's not the worst thing in the world to make mistakes.

Being Independent – I want my friends to like me, but I don't need them to. It's important to say what I think and it's not so bad if other people disagree.

I Can Do It – I can do things that are very difficult.

Growth Mindset – When I work hard and try different things to be successful, I get smarter.

Working Tough – I want things to be fun and exciting, but they don't have to be. I can stand doing things that are hard to do, boring or uncomfortable.

Giving Effort – My success comes from trying hard. It's not because I'm lucky or what I am doing is easy.

Setting Goals – I set goals to help me achieve my personal best.

Time Management – I make sure that I am on time. I plan enough time to get things done. I keep track of my assignments and I make sure I have all my materials ready to work.

Accepting Everyone – People who are different from me, people I don't know and people who do the wrong thing are not total losers. Everyone has positive qualities. Everyone deserves to be treated respectfully.

Thinking First – When people treat me unfairly or do not give me what I want, it is better to take some time to think about how to go about solving the problem and not doing the first thing that comes to mind.

Following Rules – By following important school and home rules, I will live in a world where everyone communicates freely, feels safe and enjoys learning.

When my kids were growing up, I would discuss and illustrate these attitudes explaining and showing them how each operates.

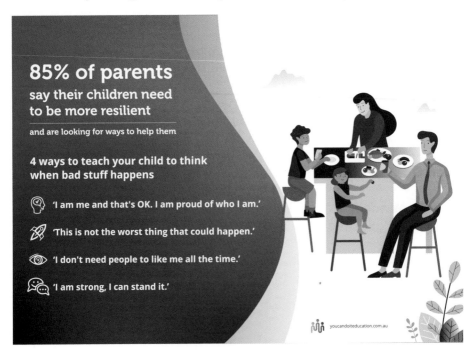

CASE STUDY. HOW I ALMOST TAUGHT MY SON THE ATTITUDE OF GIVING EFFORT

When we lived in the USA, Jonathon, seven years old, was very upset because while he was a member of the boy's Under-8 soccer team he wasn't being picked by his coach to play very much during the game. He warmed the bench a lot of the time I remember one game, Jonathon was not selected at all by his coach to play. It looked like the coach simply forgot about Jonathon. Jonathon was in tears after the game. I took him aside and explained the way I saw things. 'JD (his nickname), the reason the coach doesn't pick you to play very much is that during practice you don't seem to try very hard. You don't run as hard as you can for the ball – and you are very fast. Here's what you need to know. The more effort you put into something, the greater your chances for success. So, this coming week I want you to try as hard as you can in practice, run like the wind.' And that week, JD did as I advised – I observed him during his soccer practices. He ran, ran and ran. The next Saturday, game day, the coach put him in the game during the second quarter. I could tell by his expression he was serious in wanting to play the rest of the game. So, he ran, ran and ran – and after passing the ball to his teammate who kicked the ball back to him, JD kicked a goal! And it turned out to be the winning goal. After the game, the coach congratulated him for his effort and told JD he would be a starting member of the team for the following week. And was I proud of him – and me for offering such good advice. On the way home, I noticed a small chain sticking out above his athletic sock. 'Hey JD, what's that?' He responded, 'Oh Dad, it's a lucky rabbits foot. Mum gave it to me when she knew how upset I was about not playing very much and she said if I wore it in my sock, my luck would change. And it did!' It took the whole trip home to convince him that it was his effort more than luck that determines how things turn out.

Here are some ways you can teach your children the positive attitudes that contribute to a high performance mindset.

1. **Explain that there are different ways to think that help us to be successful and happy.**
   For example: 'The way people think about things really can help or hurt their chances of being successful and being happy. If I think "I can't do something," I am more likely to give up than if I think "I haven't learned this yet".'

2. **Pick an attitude you want to teach and provide your child with a clear understanding of what it means.**
   For example: 'A great way to think is called Working Tough which means that while you want things you have to do at school to be fun and exciting, things sometimes are not going to be that way. To be successful, you sometimes have to do things you don't feel like doing.'

3. **Model the attitude yourself.**
   For example: 'Take me at work. One thing I dislike doing and find boring is checking over my writing to make sure I haven't made any spelling errors and everything makes sense. At these times, I apply the Working Tough way of thinking. I remind myself to do a great job, I have to do the boring bits.'

4. **Reinforce your children when you catch them using the attitude you are teaching.**
   For example: 'I can see you using your Working Tough way of thinking in practising your spelling list/writing an essay. Working Tough helps you put in the effort needed to get the job done and to do your personal best.'

Social-emotional skills

In our program, You Can Do It! Education, parents are encouraged to help develop the five essential social and emotional foundations ('keys') all young people need to be successful and happy. By helping your children become more aware of and use these keys at home and in school, you are helping develop a high performance mindset.

Make sure that you take the time to explain what these five keys are and how they can be used. Each of the five keys is now briefly described including some ideas about what you can do at home to support their development.

RESILIENCE

Resilience is shown when young people are able to stop themselves from getting extremely angry, down, or worried when faced with challenging events and difficult situations and people. Resilience means being able to control your behaviour when very upset without fighting or withdrawing for too long. It also means being able to calm down after having been upset and bouncing back to work and being with other people.

Practical things you can do to help your children become resilient (calm down when extremely upset)

- Accept that it is normal and healthy for your child to experience negative emotions. (It is good to show and talk about different negative feelings you have, as long as they are not too extreme.)
- Provide your child with words to describe his/her own feelings (e.g., 'You are feeling angry.' 'You are feeling worried.' or 'You are feeling sad.') as well as your own feelings (e.g., 'I am angry you broke that....').
- Teach your child to say to themselves 'calm down' and to take three big breaths before doing something s/he finds frightening or when s/he is very angry or sad.
- Model for your child the kinds of positive self-talk s/he can use when s/he is experiencing a bad situation to help brighten his/her mood (e.g., 'This isn't so bad, it won't last forever.').

- Discuss with your child the importance of finding a grown up to talk to when s/he has very bad feelings. This could be a parent, a teacher, or a family member.
- Explain to your child that when s/he gets very upset, s/he should find something fun to do to help him/her calm down.

CONFIDENCE

Confidence requires that young people not be overly concerned with what others think if they make a mistake. Confidence is revealed when young people are not afraid to fail and are happy to meet someone new. Confidence involves young people having trust in themselves and believing that they will probably be successful in the end. Confident young people stand up straight, look people in the eye, and speak clearly and with a firm tone of voice.

Practical things you can do to develop confidence in your children

- Give your child a special responsibility (e.g., special role or job).
- Ask your child questions you know s/he can answer. Prompt him/her before asking question so s/he is prepared and experiences success.
- Set aside time each day for your child to demonstrate what s/he has learned at school.
- Help your child to identify and develop individual interests and talents by showing interest in and excitement about areas of your young child's skills and talents.
- Do not give your child too much attention when he/she expresses negative feelings about schoolwork.
- Encourage your child to speak up when asked a question.
- Encourage your child to have eye contact with adults (if appropriate to your culture) or others when being spoken to.
- Practise asking your child his/her name and age so that he/she can respond with a confident, clear voice.
- Provide your child with many opportunities to do things where s/he can be successful. Provide praise at these times.
- Praise your child for trying something new.

Persistence is revealed when young people try hard when doing schoolwork, they find frustrating and do not feel like doing and finish their work on time. Young people who keep trying to complete an assignment rather than becoming distracted, and those who elect to play after they've done their work, demonstrate motivation and can be described as being persistent.

Practical things you can do to develop persistence in your children

- Provide your child with accurate feedback concerning the amount of effort s/he is expending and how much effort and time is really needed to complete a task such as a puzzle or a drawing.
- Discuss with your child repeatedly how his/her big effort results in learning or success.
- Provide strong, immediate reinforcement (i.e., verbal and non-verbal) for effort your child puts toward work that s/he finds hard or boring (little jobs, puzzle, colouring).
- Praise your child when s/he willingly does tasks (chores) that are not fun without complaining.
- Catch your child doing something that requires effort and praise him/her for trying hard.
- Praise your child for returning to a task (chore) that requires effort to complete.

Organisation is revealed when young people keep track of their assignments, schedule their time effectively, break down long-term assignments into small steps and set goals for how well they want to do in specific areas of their schoolwork and in other endeavours. Organisation also means having all supplies ready to do schoolwork and a good system for storing previously learned material.

Practical things you can do to develop organisation in your children

- Provide your child with simple instructions regarding how to organise his/her toys, play area, and the bag s/he takes to school.
- Establish a routine and schedule for your young child to perform the necessary daily needs, e.g., teeth brushing before bedtime reading, eating breakfast before playing or watching TV, putting things away when finished using them.
- Establish a set routine at home for wake-up time, being dressed and ready to leave, dinner time, ready for bedtime, and sleep.
- Only provide materials your child needs for current work/play.
- Allow time before leaving home, the park, to collect his/her things or help put things away.
- Ensure that your child is ready for instructions (e.g., eye contact, sitting still) when explaining a task to him/her.
- Teach your child ways to remember directions and instructions (e.g., red canister holds the biscuits).

GETTING ALONG

Getting Along is revealed when young people work cooperatively with each other, resolve conflicts by discussion rather than fights, manage their anger, show tolerance, and follow school and home rules and expectations, including making responsible choices so that everyone's rights are protected. Getting Along also involves young people making positive contributions to helping others and to making the school, home, and community safer, healthier, and good places to live and learn.

Practical things you can do to help your children get along

- Acknowledge and praise your young child when s/he is demonstrating good getting along skills.
- Do not use sarcasm, put your child down, communicate with a negative tone of voice, or become furious when your child misbehaves.
- Teach your child what to say when s/he meets someone new (introduce himself/herself by name, say 'hello', smile).
- Teach your child to take turns when playing.

- Teach your child the importance of telling the truth, not saying mean things to someone else, and doing something nice for someone who has hurt feelings or is sad.
- Avoid placing your child together with a child who does not get along well with others.
- Provide opportunities for your child to share his/her toys with another child. Then praise your child for doing so.
- Provide opportunities for your child to experience taking turns with someone when doing something s/he likes to do. Acknowledge his/her patience in waiting his/her turn.
- Always communicate in a friendly, kind manner with your child.

PARENT EDUCATION

I keep learning more about what research says about how to be a positive parent and what my friends have offered in terms of support and guidance along the way. And in my professional work, I've

written a lot about what works and what doesn't work at home. I also have been invited to present talks to parent groups on different topics.

If parent education is of interest because of your role in a school, have a look at Investing in Parents – a series of parent education sessions that you can present to groups of parents covering a lot of the information on parenting presented in this part of the book (youcandoiteducation.com.au/parents).

Investing in Parents
(parent education classes to offer at your school)

MICHAEL E BERNARD, PHD
PROFESSOR, MELBOURNE GRADUATE SCHOOL OF EDUCATION
UNIVERSITY OF MELBOURNE
EMERITUS PROFESSOR, CALIFORNIA STATE UNIVERSITY, LONG BEACH
FOUNDER, YOU CAN DO IT! EDUCATION

You Can Do It!
Education

Patricia and I have developed one of the first online, positive, parent education programs that is a great source of video programs and digital articles on many ways to be a positive and effective parent including how to raise positive kids.

We hope this part of the book has left you with new ideas to share with your family.

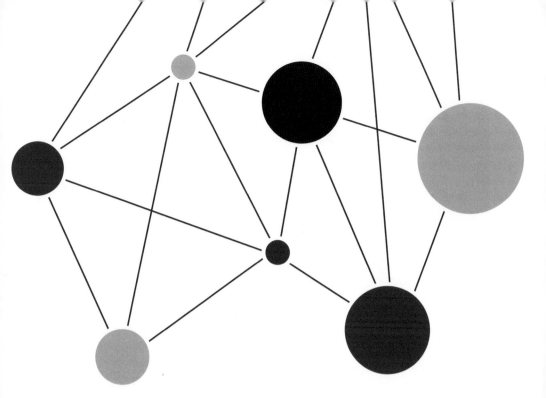

Part 7

Life

'How can you make yourself happy? Increased happiness and freedom from disturbance can be achieved because all humans are born with constructive and creative tendencies and born with the ability to sharpen and increase their self-fulfilling tendencies... Rational beliefs bring us closer to getting good results in the real world.'
- Albert Ellis, author, *How to Stubbornly Refuse to Make Yourself Upset About Anything, Yes Anything!*

'People take different roads seeking fulfillment and happiness. Just because they're not on your road doesn't mean they've gotten lost.'
- Dalai Lama, spiritual leader of the Tibetan people

'Strive for the long-range pleasure of tomorrow as well as the short-term satisfaction of today.'
- Albert Ellis, author, *A New Guide to Rational Living*

'Most people are searching for happiness. They're looking for it. They're trying to find it in someone or something outside of themselves. That's a fundamental mistake. Happiness is something that you are, and it comes from the way you think.'
- Wayne Dyer, author, *Your Erroneous Zones*

RATIONALITY AND THE PURSUIT OF HAPPINESS

'Planning your personal happiness is an enormous, challenging task that pits you against some of the most powerful forces in the universe. For as Voltaire sagely noted, this is not the best of all possible worlds. Life is filled with a constant series of muddles and puddles. It is not, as we teach horrible and awful; but it is frequently a royal pain in the ass. And if you actively seek happiness, you mean that you will fully accept the challenge of this difficult existence and will be utterly determined to make it less difficult for you personally and, in fact, damned exciting and enjoyable.' Albert Ellis and Irving Becker, *A Guide to Personal happiness*

To live a very happy and fulfilled life, your outer world in terms of your economic status, education and social-family support is important.

Your *inner world*, your mindset, however, essential in two basic ways.

First, your mindset needs to be able to prevent and overcome social and emotional problems that you can experience like anxiety, feeling down or anger that blocks you in your search for short-term fun and satisfaction as well as long-term fulfilment.

Second, your mindset also needs to be able direct you towards experiences that have the potential to release your potential and which develop you as a person.

What can greatly assist you to overcome social-emotional issues and to be self-actualising is a faculty of mind, *rationality*.

Rationality does not mean without feeling. Emotions are a natural part of human experience that we need to learn more about ourselves and to grow. Rationality means we are sensible and objective in the way we think about, interpret and evaluate our experiences. Rationality means we experience healthy, negative emotions such as extreme concern, annoyance and sadness when confronted with life's hassles and adversity. Rationality also means as much as possible, our behaviour helps us to achieve the goals we set in the short- and long-term.

In my early years as a practising psychologist, I saw how mindset contributes to and often causes a range of mental health problems. This was after all the dawning of the cognitive revolution in the field of psychotherapy where leaders such as Aaron Beck (Cognitive Therapy) and Albert Ellis (Rational Emotive Behavior Therapy) wrote about how people can overcome their emotional difficulties by becoming aware of and making changes to errors in their thinking as well as re-structuring their irrational beliefs to rational beliefs.

I was so fortunate to have been introduced to and mentored by Albert Ellis. Over the years, I visited Ellis at his Institute in New York City many times including spending one full year there as a research scientist. I learnt so much from him as I sat in on his group therapy sessions.

Ellis lent me over 100 of his audio recordings of his best REBT therapy sessions and public lectures where he taught the basics of REBT to help people overcome all problems under the sun. One year I devoted myself to listening to Ellis' tapes, had the more powerful interchanges between Ellis and a client transcribed so others could learn from the master and published a book written foreveryone, *Staying Rational In an Irrational World*.

Albert Ellis at Michael Bernard's book launch

Ellis agreed with Karen Horney, a German-born psychoanalyst who described the 'tyranny of the shoulds' – the rigid and unrealistic expectations that people hold about themselves that she asserted where the true cause of anxiety. Ellis also was a voracious reader of philosophers such as Marcus Aurelius and Epictetus who wrote that 'People are not effected by events, but by their views of events.'

Ellis proposed that most mental health issues were not caused by early childhood experiences and upbringing nor by people's immediate environment. Rather, Ellis declared that people's beliefs – the way they looked at and interpreted their world – held the answer to why people became disturbed about their world.

Ellis developed REBT as a system for understanding people of all ages and helping them to overcome mental health issues through helping them become aware of what he called 'irrational beliefs' and how to change them to 'rational beliefs'.

Here are the irrational beliefs that Ellis proposed are the basis of mental health problems, and their rational alternatives.

Irrational Belief 1. *I must do well and win approval or else I am an inadequate, rotten person.*
Rational alternative (USA - Unconditional Self-Acceptance): *Accept your self, essence, totality whether you act and perform well and whether or not you are approved of by significant others. Under all conditions!*

Irrational Belief 2. *Others must act considerately and kindly in precisely the way I want them to treat me; if they don't, society and the universe should severely blame, damn and punish them for their inconsiderateness.*
Rational alternative (UOA – Unconditional Other-Acceptance): *Accept, respect, honour and love your partner and others even with their shortcomings and failings. Strongly see and feel the Christian idea to accept the sinner but not the sin.*

Irrational Belief 3. *Conditions under which I live must be arranged so that I get practically everything that I want comfortably, quickly and easily and get virtually nothing that I don't want.*
Rational alternative (ULA – Unconditional Life Acceptance or High Frustration Tolerance): *Accept life with its hassles, problems and difficulties. Create enjoyment in it for yourself and others; not always, but fairly consistently.*

I co-founded the Australian Institute for Rational Emotive Therapy with a colleague, Dr. Ian Campbell, and over the years we trained hundreds of mental health practitioners in how to employ REBT with people of all ages. For seven years, I was the Editor-in-Chief of the Journal of Rational-Emotive, Cognitive-Behavior Therapy. Patricia and I coordinated two visits by Ellis to Australia where he offered workshops to professional and talks for the general public (1,300 people attended one of his evening talks at the Camberwell Civic Centre). I was honoured to be appointed as a Fellow of the Institute for Rational Emotive Therapy (now the Albert Ellis Institute) and am an approved supervisor of therapists in training.

In the early part of my professional career, I worked in schools as a school psychologist using REBT with young people who were referred to me with a variety of mental health issues like anxiety, depression and anger as well as poor motivation and under-achievement. I applied Ellis' theories and practices showing young people how their thinking was often the culprit and by changing their thinking, they could produce a dramatic change in how they felt about themselves, family members, peers, school and the world. I was blown away by how powerful REBT was in helping young people – as I am today

I authored with my good friend, Marie Joyce, one of the first books on using REBT with young people.

Here's what a 14-year old with low self-esteem and who was under-achieving wrote about REBT:

'That before coming here, everything that went wrong I used to blame it on myself. I used to say I was no good at anything, and why don't I just kill myself. I didn't know the meaning of Rational and Erational thoughts – they have slowly changed the way I think, so I don't get so upset as I used to. I used to think of my bad points but now I also think of my good points, so now I don't go off my rocker, I am lucky to be able to think Rational thoughts.'

I have been equally interested in understanding how rationality can contribute to positive emotions and high levels of happiness and satisfaction.

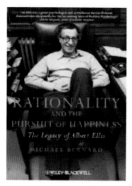

Martin Seligman, the founder of the field of Positive Psychology in the year 2000, recognised the contribution of Albert Ellis to the field of positive psychology when he wrote the following testimony for my book, *Rationality and the Pursuit of Happiness*:

'Al Ellis was a great psychologist and as Professor Bernard's book demonstrates eloquently, he was an unsung hero of positive psychology.'

Ellis and his associates wrote many books for the general public on the ABCs of happiness including with Robert Harper, A New Guide to Rational Living, and with Irving Becker, A Guide to Personal Happiness. Ellis' guides to rational living encourage people to experiment with their lifestyle, make choices of what to spend one's life doing based on personal knowledge and discovery that would bring them higher levels of excitement, passion, pleasure and zest in the short-term as well as pleasure, satisfaction and fulfilment in the long-term.

As a result of my work with Albert Ellis, teaching many, many people over the years about how to overcome their social and emotional problems with rationality and to chart a course towards happiness and life fulfilment, I have some things to offer in this last part of the book.

SELF-ACCEPTANCE

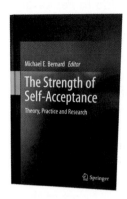

Michael E. Bernard *Editor*

The Strength of Self-Acceptance

Theory, Practice and Research

Springer

I am so convinced that self-acceptance is a cornerstone of mental health happiness and fulfilment that several years ago I edited one of the first books on the topic. Self-acceptance is not only needed to prevent and overcome social-emotional difficulties but to enjoy oneself in the short-term and live a fulfilled life in the long-term. FOR SURE!

I have found that the absence of self-acceptance as part of one's core belief system and mindset makes it very hard to be emotionally healthy and leads to a range of social-emotional blockers like anxiety and depression.

Many mentally healthy people are happy to be alive and accept themselves because they are alive and can enjoy themselves. They refuse to measure their intrinsic worth by their extrinsic achievement of what others think of them. As much as possible, they accept themselves unconditionally and they try to completely avoid rating themselves. They try to enjoy life rather than prove themselves.

Are you someone who when faced with strong criticism, failures, setbacks or significant lack of success **AVOIDS** giving yourself a general, overall negative rating such as, 'I'm hopeless', but instead, believes you are still a worthwhile person, thinking, 'I accept myself no matter what'?

If so, you demonstrate *self-acceptance* which is, perhaps, the most important of all attitudes underpinning your mental health.

Conversely, *self-depreciation* is an attitude that is a primary cause of emotional difficulties and mental health disorders like depression and anxiety.

Self-acceptance means acknowledging that you are a complex, imperfect human being capable of making mistakes as well as significant accomplishments. You possess a realistic awareness of your strengths and weaknesses. You accept yourself in spite of your imperfections and because of your uniqueness. You refrain from self-criticism, avoiding rating your self-worth based on other people thinking negatively of what you do, the way you look, or when you perceive you do not live up to your own expectations.

Being clear on self-acceptance

Self-acceptance is not an excuse for accepting your bad or inappropriate behaviour. In fact, with strong self-acceptance, it is much easier to realistically evaluate what you do and to work on changing behaviour that is inappropriate or self-defeating.

Self-acceptance is not self-esteem. Self-esteem refers to our judgments about how much we like or value ourselves and is based on comparisons with others and on the extent to which we achieve personal goals.

Not taking things personally gives you the resilience, confidence and wisdom to change those things about yourself that need changing and the calmness to accept those things that you cannot change.

Self-acceptance at work

Steve, a promising teacher known for innovative student engagement methods, has taken a job as a science and technology teacher at a large, established secondary school. After a few months of teaching, his Head of Department has begun being quite critical of his pedagogy. Additionally, his Head has taken to sarcastically criticising his ideas presented at team meetings. Steve is effectively managing the emotional impact of the highly critical interactions. How? He reminds himself that while his Head's behaviour is not acceptable, with strong self-acceptance he refuses to take it personally. As a consequence, he more readily copes with it. Steve's calmness in the line of fire not only helps maintain his mental health and wellbeing, it also gives him the breathing space to see what, if anything, he can do to change the way his Head communicates.

Lack of self-acceptance is harmful to your mental health

When we are confronted with criticism/rejection by a significant other or when we're faced with a lack of success in performing an important task, we can think of ourselves as a failure or hopeless. This is called self-depreciation. This negative attitude literally causes feelings of depression and anxiety.

Self-depreciation represents an extreme form of thinking that is not based on evidence. When you think you are a total loser or failure, you are in essence saying there is no evidence in any area of your life that you are capable of anything at all, or likeable by anyone. This is highly unlikely to be true! Self-depreciation is illogical due to its' over-generalisation; that is, one or more negative aspects of you or your behaviour simply does not mean that ALL aspects of you are negative.

All of us, to a greater or lesser extent, have a tendency to devalue ourselves and to take things personally. This is due in part to our early childhood and continuing life experiences as well as our innate temperament.

Beliefs about self-worth are the most difficult to change. Fortunately, armed with self-awareness and tools for changing self-belief, most people can be taught how to overcome this tendency.

The key insight for change is knowing that you do, in fact, have the power to choose self-acceptance or not.

How strong is my self-acceptance?

Here are some descriptors of low self-acceptance.

The more you agree with these statements, the more likely it is that you have low self-acceptance:

- ✓ Saying something stupid in front of others shows I am an idiot.
- ✓ I am someone who needs my friends to like me in order for me to feel important and worthwhile.
- ✓ When a colleague treats me unfairly, I think I must be useless.
- ✓ I feel I always must do well in important tasks and activities.
- ✓ When a friend asks others but not me to join him/her, I can't help but think I'm a loser.
- ✓ When I don't succeed at something in my work that is important to me, I am likely to think I'm a complete failure.
- ✓ When I don't experience exciting times with others, I think I'm a dull and uninteresting person.
- ✓ I am someone who needs to perform well to feel important and worthwhile.

Keys for strengthening your self-acceptance

1. It is important to distinguish between being a failure and failing at a task. YOU are not your behaviour.

2. People's opinions of you are not facts. If someone says you are a totally useless piece of garbage does that make it true?

3. Be aware of and value your positive characteristics, skills and character strengths in all areas of life including work and family relationships – do not take these strengths for granted. Then, when faced with difficulty or negativity, remind yourself why you are proud of who you are.

4. Generate and practice using self-accepting self-talk when confronted with criticism, imperfect performance, negative self-perceptions of body image or other events you experience as troubling.
   - ✓ 'I accept myself no matter what.'
   - ✓ 'I prefer people to like me, but I can live without their approval.'
   - ✓ 'Mistakes and setbacks are inevitable. I will accept myself while disliking my mistakes and setbacks.'
   - ✓ 'My performance at work – perfect or otherwise – does not determine my worth as a person.'
   - ✓ 'I accept who I am, even though I may not like some of my traits and behaviours.'

5. Rating your overall self-worth as poor, based on negative results or what others think of you, does not make sense. Use the following analogy developed by Albert Ellis next time you feel down about yourself to challenge and change self-depreciation to self-acceptance:

    Imagine that you have just received a large basket of fruit. You reach into the basket and pull out a beautiful red apple, and then a ripe, juicy pear, but then you find a rotten orange, followed by a perfect banana, and then a bunch of grapes, some of which are mushy and rotten. Clearly, some pieces are good and some are not so good. How would you label the basket or judge its overall value? You see, the basket represents you, and the variety of fruits which vary in ripeness are like your traits, strengths and weaknesses. Rating yourself overall, based on a single trait is like saying that the basket of fruit is totally bad and worthless, just because it contains a few pieces of bad fruit.

Young People's Self-Acceptance

How important is self-acceptance to the happiness and general life satisfaction to not only grown-ups but for young people? Beyond Blue, an Australian national organisation working to address issues associated with depression, suicide, anxiety disorders and other related mental disorders has recently published an Information Sheet I authored on Self-Acceptance.

My research on self-acceptance in young people shows that high levels contribute to positive emotions and satisfaction in life whereas low levels are associated with negative emotions and emotional difficulties.

Self-Acceptance: The Psychological 'Armour' that Protects Young People

SELF-ACCEPTANCE inoculates and protects young people to deal with stressful situations, such as poor achievement, negative peer comments, issues with body image, identity and other developmental challenges and difficulties. Awareness of this fact is central to the alleviation of social-emotional problems of young people as well to the promotion of high levels of life satisfaction and wellbeing.

Self-acceptance in young people means they possess a realistic awareness of their strengths and weaknesses. They accept themselves despite imperfections and because of their uniqueness. They refrain from self-criticism, avoiding rating their self-worth based on other people thinking negatively of what they do, the way they look and/or when they feel they do not live up to their own expectations.

Why self-acceptance in young people must be addressed

Chronic depression and high anxiety results from the attitude of self-depreciation and a lack of strong self-acceptance. Due to social and developmental factors, many young people feel badly about themselves.

To combat young people's tendencies to self-depreciate, parents and teachers can help young people to not rate their self-worth based on their achievements, what others think of them, or their body image, but rather to display 'self-acceptance' – regardless of external factors.

Research shows that when young people with depression and anxiety receive cognitive, rational emotive behaviour therapies that replace the dysfunctional attitude of self-depreciation with self-acceptance, their mental health improves.

Self-acceptance in young people – what it looks like

Two girls receive the same text message on several occasions saying that each looks FAT and UGLY. Carmen is quite devastated; feeling extremely anxious and depressed about the impact of the message on her popularity, while Alex pays little attention to the message, reminds herself that she is a worthwhile person, and returns an SMS saying that the sender should have paid more attention in their recent health class on celebrating differences and not judging people by their appearance, culture or behaviour.

The emotional impact of this cyber-bullying event is dramatically different for the two girls because of the different attitude or mindset of each girl. As a consequence of her attitude of self-depreciation, Carmen takes being cyberbullied quite personally thinking, 'Because I am being picked on for my physical appearance, there must be something wrong with me. I now think less of myself and I must be a real loser'.

In contrast, Alex's attitude of self-acceptance literally protects her. She refuses to rate her self-worth and value based on another's opinion of her, instead thinking, 'I accept myself no matter what' and 'I am me and that's OK.'

The pressure is on kids

The research indicates that 50% of young people today say they feel very stressed compared with 30% in 2003.

Social media isn't helping, with young people constantly being shown what it means to be successful, physically attractive and cool. A myriad of mobile devices makes it that much easier to tease and bully – and get away with it. Young people feel they are constantly being judged, requiring 'likes' and other people's approval just to feel worthwhile. Our kids are doing all they can to live up to and meet their peer's expectations.

Plus, there is a ton of pressure on young people from parents and teachers to perform well in school.

Many parents today are very anxious about their children. Consequently, many parents are over-protecting their children, with the result being that many young people feel very vulnerable and lack resilience, partly because they do not possess strong self-acceptance.

Research facts

- 58% of young people worry excessively about what others think of them.
- 35% say that when they do badly in their schoolwork, they think 'I'm a failure.'
- In primary and secondary schools, student self-acceptance is associated with positive emotions and high levels of life satisfaction.
- In primary and secondary schools, student self-depreciation is associated with negative emotions and low levels of life satisfaction.
- Student self-depreciation, anxiety and anger are often seen alongside behavioural problems and teacher ratings of students' low effort in school.

Child developmental considerations

Fortunately, many very young children (3–6 years.) tend to perceive themselves in a very favourable light. However, those that experience a high incidence of negative encounters with other people and with their learning, can be heard thinking aloud: 'I'm a loser,' 'I'm hopeless' and 'I'm a bad kid.' By the age of eight, these negative self-evaluations can become internalised, automatic and pervasive.

Children in middle to late childhood (8–10 years.) are more at risk for developing negative self-evaluations than younger children. Due to their increasing abilities to see themselves through the eyes of others as well as be concerned by the discrepancy between the way they would like to be (ideal self) and the way they really are (real self), they demonstrate great vulnerability to self-depreciation and low self-esteem.

Adolescents bring additional challenges with adolescent egocentrism emerging in 11–13-year-olds. The way they view themselves may be very unrealistic. Their construction of an imaginary audience reflects the false assumption that others, particularly peers, are as preoccupied with their behavior and appearance as they are, and that peers are constantly submitting them to scrutiny and critical evaluation. While academic achievements are also important to self-evaluations, perceptions of physical appearance top the list in terms of the correlation with feelings of overall self-worth. During this stage, because of an increase in negative self-evaluations, physical development, hormones, timing of puberty, and an increase in stressful life events, depression rates rise from 2–5% to 8%.

Implications for school culture, policy and leadership

Schools and staff need to explicitly incorporate self-acceptance throughout school culture and practice as applied to themselves, students and through parent education. This means, as a staff, taking time to become aware of what self-acceptance is and reflecting on their own degree of self-acceptance and ways it can be modelled for students. Then, as a staff, identifying opportunities to bring students on board including presenting on self-acceptance at assemblies; revealing to students that they have choices in how they think when they are faced with difficulty and challenges; and explaining the differences between self-acceptance, self-depreciation and the emotional consequences of each.

Incorporating self-acceptance in behaviour management practice and in teachable moments when students are faced with stressful situations, like tasks that are difficult or bullying incidents, is very important. And, for students receiving counselling and individual support, self-acceptance needs to be foundational.

School SEL programs for strengthening self-acceptance in children and young people

In You Can Do It! Education, we have developed and refined lessons that teachers can use to explicitly teach self-acceptance and self-downing which appear in:

You Can Do It! Early Childhood Program Achieve, 3rd Ed
https://edu.youcandoiteducation.com.au/blocks/androgogic_catalogue/index.php?id=6

NEW Program Achieve (years 1-6; years 7-12). A social-emotional learning curriculum
https://edu.youcandoiteducation.com.au/blocks/androgogic_catalogue/index.php?id=1
https://edu.youcandoiteducation.com.au/blocks/androgogic_catalogue/index.php?id=7

Sample titles of lessons include: Getting Up when Feeling Down; What to Do When You are Feeling Down; Accept Myself No Matter

What; Feeling Down? Don't Take Things Personally; Feeling Down. Be Proud of You

School-home practices for strengthening self-acceptance in children and young people

For younger children (less than eight years.), the path to strong self-acceptance is paved by parents, teachers and significant others through:

- Encouraging them to make positive, realistic judgements of how smart they are, their physical abilities, how they look and behave
- Being proud of their achievements
- Providing evidence and discussion about when they learn new things that are hard, through their effort and trying new ways to do things, they become smarter and better learners
- Not judging them by their behaviour and what they have or have not accomplished
- Encouraging them to not compare their achievements with others
- When faced with difficulty and challenges, modelling self-acceptance self-talk by thinking out loud, 'I am me and that's ok. I am still proud of who I am.'
- Teaching self-talk that adults can rehearse with younger children when they are faced with difficulty in learning new skills or being treated badly by a peer:
  - 'Just because those kids don't want me to play doesn't mean I'm a total loser.'
  - 'Some kids take longer than others to learn to read. I just need to keep practising and I know I'll get there.'
  - 'Just because they called me a loser doesn't mean it's true. I know I'm not a total loser and that's the most important thing.'

As children mature, the following practices can be employed by teachers and parents to promote self-acceptance.

Practice 1. Introduce young people to self-acceptance
Say that self-acceptance can help you to think and feel positive, confident and resilient when faced with tough situations like being teased or not achieving a result you hoped for. Explain the meaning of self-acceptance: 'Accepting yourself as a worthwhile person no matter what – and being proud of who you are.' Explain that self-downing or self-depreciation means thinking untrue, unhelpful

things, such as that you are totally hopeless or a failure when you haven't been successful, someone is behaving poorly towards you or you do not like aspects of your body image.

Practice 2. Communicate unconditional positive regard

When disciplining or critiquing, do so without negative attitude or hostility. Focus on the young person's behaviour and try not to make him/her feel bad about him/herself as a person because of lack of achievement or poor behaviour.

Practice 3. Illustrate how self-acceptance can help young people deal with difficulty

If a child makes an error on an art project and begins to cry, the teacher or parent could help the child cope with the situation of making a mistake and rehearse statements such as, 'We all make mistakes, but just because we made a mistake does not mean that we are bad'. If a child becomes upset due to a physical impairment, rehearsing self-acceptance statements could include, 'I don't like that I need hearing aids, but it doesn't make me any less awesome and it's not going to stop me from coming to school.'

Practice 4. Challenge and change the young person's self-downing thinking

For example, if a young person is down in the dumps, say: 'One good way to think when you've had a bit of a setback is to remind yourself of your good points and not to put yourself down.'
Use an analogy. Ask: 'Would you trash an entire car if it had just one flat tyre?'
When young people can see that it would not make sense to do so, you can help them begin to see that trashing him or herself when one bad thing happens does not make sense either.

Practice 5. Help young people become aware of and appreciate their positive qualities

To develop young people's sense of positive self-regard, have them take stock of their individual positive skills, strengths and personality traits, including, and aside from, school performance.

Practice 6. Review with young people examples of self-accepting thinking (self-talk)

Here are examples of self-accepting self-talk that can be discussed with young people for dealing with difficult situations and events:

Happening: You get a C – in English
Self-Talk: 'Let's try and get more out of the next exam and do more practice. My value as a person is not decided by a test/exam score.'

Happening: Being excluded from a game
Self-Talk: 'I can cope with being excluded; it doesn't mean I am a loser. I am who I am, I'm still proud of whom I am. I don't need to be included in a game to feel good about myself, to be a worthwhile people.'

Summary: Communicate the psychological armour that protects

Teach children to never rate themselves in terms of their behaviour and to separate judgments of their actions from judgments of self-worth. Encourage them to acknowledge and accept responsibility for their traits and behaviours – both good and bad – without evaluating themselves as good or bad. Help combat children's tendencies towards self-downing by reminding them they are made up of many good qualities (and some that are not so good) and that they do not lose their good qualities when bad things happen. Explain to children that all human beings are capable and likeable in their unique ways and, therefore, it is good for children to accept themselves unconditionally.

RATIONAL BELIEFS FOR LIFE

All people are born with a potential to lead fulfilling and happy lives. This potential is what some call *self-actualisation*, the innate biological process all humans possess to grow and become fully functioning. With *self-actualisation*, people possess the innate desire to utilise their unique aptitudes and constructive, creative problem solving tendencies that orient them towards doing things that bring them enjoyment and fulfillment.

However, the self-actualising potential can be blocked by emotional difficulties as well as inertia – the tendency to sit around and do nothing rather than actively participating in diverse activities to discover those that do (and do not) bring enjoyment and happiness.

Due to biological make-up and early childhood experiences, the self-actualising process operates in different people at various strengths depending on their life circumstances, emotional health and willpower to overcome inertia.

Rationality is a potent force to help people achieve their goals of long life and happiness. Albert Ellis enumerated a set of *beliefs of rational living* that when people put into practice on a regular basis can have impressive effects on their self-actualisation and resultant personal happiness.

In order to be happy and experience fewer emotional lows, you will want to practice rational beliefs as often as possible. As Albert Ellis said in his *New Guide to Rational Living*, rational beliefs bring us closer to getting good results in the real world.

The accompanying *Rationality and Happiness Survey* can assist you in identifying those rational beliefs you wish to incorporate into your high performance mindset.

RATIONALITY AND HAPPINESS SURVEY

The following survey has been used by many people to help in their search for increased personal happiness. I hope you will find it of benefit.

Instructions: Consider the following list of Rational Beliefs. Indicate how often you put each one into practice.

Self-interest

There is an inalienable right of all human beings to be happy.

Don't always sacrifice yourself to meet the needs of others.

Make time for enjoying yourself.

Rather than spending all of my time in meeting the needs of others, I make a point of spending some of my time doing things I find interesting and enjoyable.

☐ Seldom
☐ Sometimes
☐ Often

Social interest

Be respectful and caring.

Volunteer to help others.

In exploring my interests, I make sure that my actions do not hurt others or interfere with their rights. I treat others with respect. I become involved. I am helping others.

☐ Seldom
☐ Sometimes
☐ Often

Self-direction

Plan for experiences you predict will bring you happiness.

Solve problems as they emerge.

Minimise those activities that bring you displeasure.

I do not wait around for other people (family, work, government) to do things to make me happy. Rather, I actively plan for those experiences that I think will bring me pleasure and satisfaction. I also make decisions about those activities that bring me displeasure and see if they can be shared or minimised.

☐ Seldom
☐ Sometimes
☐ Often

Self-acceptance

Eliminate self-depreciation.

Accept yourself as a fallible human being.

When I have not been successful in important tasks at work or have been criticised or rejected by someone whose opinion I value, I do not put myself down or take it personally.

☐ Seldom
☐ Sometimes
☐ Often

Tolerance of others

Extreme anger blocks happiness.

Accept all sinners but not their sins.

When someone behaves unfairly or disrespectfully, I am able to keep separate the person's negative behaviour and actions from my overall judgment of their value or worth as a person.

☐ Seldom
☐ Sometimes
☐ Often

Short and long term hedonism

Enjoy yourself today but not at the expense of achieving what you want in the long-term.

While I enjoy immediate gratification (fun, pleasure, excitement), I also have a clear focus on what I want to achieve in the long term in order to be satisfied with my work, health and family life. I balance time spent having fun with the hard work and sacrifice needed to achieve my longer-term goals.

☐ Seldom
☐ Sometimes
☐ Often

Commitment to creative, absorbing activities and pursuits

Discover activities that enable you to exercise your creativity...

... and to become absorbed in what you do!

I make a real effort to discover activities that are fun and exciting and when practised over an extended period result in fulfilment. When I discover what I am interested in, I commit energy to the activity.

☐ Seldom
☐ Sometimes
☐ Often

Risk taking and experimenting

Experiment with many tasks and projects to discover what you enjoy.

Keep risking defeats and failures.

In order to find experiences that bring me heightened or new enjoyments, I experiment with many tasks and projects to discover what I really want. I am prepared to step out of my comfort zone and I am willing to risk defeat or rejection.

☐ Seldom
☐ Sometimes
☐ Often

High frustration tolerance and will power

Make a decision to change and follow it up with action.

Tolerate frustration and discomfort. To exercise your will power.

When I make a decision about something I want to do that can bring me success at work, enrich a relationship, or improve my health, I follow up with hard work and effort no matter the degree of frustration or discomfort.

☐ Seldom
☐ Sometimes
☐ Often

Problem solving

Practical problems are those that you experience with your outside world.

When I am faced with a problem at work or home, I apply methods that help to solve the problem.

☐ Seldom
☐ Sometimes
☐ Often

Scientific thinking and flexibility

Be scientific in considering the evidence as to what really brings you happiness.

Eliminate un-scientific, irrational thinking.

I do not solely rely on the opinion of others about the way I should do things. I am open minded and evaluate ways to live my life based on my experiences and opportunities. When I am in a rut or things are not working out, I am flexible in changing the way I do things.

☐ Seldom
☐ Sometimes
☐ Often

So, as a personal philosophy of happiness, a rational mindset sounds to me something like this.

✓ I have a right to be happy and to search for pursuits and experiences that are pleasurable to me in the short-term and fulfilling in the long-term. There is no point in waiting around for happiness to find me.

✓ While I have a right to take this journey, I will take responsibility for ensuring that I do not cause needless harm to others in my social and family group. In fact, by committing myself to the welfare of others, I frequently will live a more satisfying life.

✓ Now, as I am a fallible human being, when confronted by my imperfections or people's negative judgments of me and my behaviour, I will as often as possible choose not to put myself down but instead accept myself.

✓ I will also choose not to rate the worth or overall value of people who do the wrong thing or whose customs or behaviour I dislike. Instead, I will make a concerted effort to learn more about them as people.

✓ I know that I will be happier and more fulfilled when I take risks and experiment to become involved in creative and absorbing activities. While I will seek out short-term pleasures, I will not sacrifice long-term gains of sustained commitments by becoming overly focussed on immediate short-term gratification.

✓ When I am confronted with inevitable misfortune and life's frustrations, I will use scientific thinking to manage my emotional responses so that I do not rigidly obsess and demand that things be different than they are – while trying hard to make the changes that I can, the serenity to accept those things I cannot change, and the wisdom to know the difference.

✓ I will work at becoming a successful problem solver of life's practical problems and when problems do not go away, figuring out ways that I can still be happy. I also understand that I need to work hard at thinking rationally about my life's difficulties so that I do not become desperately unhappy and I need to rely on my willpower to overcome inertia that can impede my discovering those pursuits that bring me happiness.

Final words

Only by working at, planning and acting at it are you likely to become more fully self-actualised and live a happy and fulfilled life.

It is good to be optimistic but not unrealistic about your potential for greater happiness through rationality. Rationality is no miracle cure but you can have confidence it may work.

Keep in mind that it has helped millions of people over the decades to live LIFE to its fullest.

In concluding this book, thanks for picking it up. Its' been an honour and privilege to share with you some of my life's journey, stories and what I have learnt over the years personally and professionally. I hope you are taking away more than one idea that will make a difference to your work, home and life. **ONWARDS!**